How To Keep Your
Tractor Running

How To Keep Your
Tractor Running

Rick Kubik

MOTORBOOKS

First published in 2005 by Motorbooks, an imprint of MBI Publishing Company, Galtier Plaza, Suite 200, 380 Jackson Street, St. Paul, MN 55101-3885 USA

Motorbooks titles are also available at discounts in bulk quantity for industrial or sales-promotional use. For details write to Special Sales Manager at MBI Publishing Company, Galtier Plaza, Suite 200, 380 Jackson Street, St. Paul, MN 55101-3885 USA.

Library of Congress Cataloging-in-Publication Data

Kubik, Rick, 1953–
　　How to keep your tractor running / by Rick Kubik.
　　　　p. cm. — (Motorbooks workshop)
　　Includes index.
　　ISBN-13: 978-0-7603-2274-1
　　ISBN-10: 0-7603-2274-0
　　　　1. Farm Tractors—Maintenance and repair. I. Title. II. Series.

TL233.2.K83 2005
631.3'72'0288—dc22
　　　　　　　　　　　　　　　　　　2005053122

On the front cover, main: This John Deere 4450 is in top running order.

Inset: This air filter needs to be replaced

On the back cover: To make your own gasket place the sheet over the part to be sealed and gently tap on the sheet to transfer the pattern to the sheet.

About the author: Rick Kubik is a certified crop adviser for the American Society of Agronomy and lives in Strathmore, Alberta, Canada.

Editor: Amy Glaser
Designer: LeAnn Kuhlmann

Printed in China

CONTENTS

INTRODUCTION

The last decade has witnessed a remarkable increase of interest in old and antique tractors. However, many of the enthusiast books about older tractors emphasize factory-correct paint schemes and decal placement or information about where and when the machine was built. At the other end of the tractor-book spectrum, technical manuals often focus on complex mechanical issues such as big end–bearing clearances, fuel-injection pump settings, and other complex things that few tractors users ever tackle. Either way, it's of little use to the owner who just wants to keep his or her tractor running. This book fills that gap. It focuses on practical knowledge for keeping that old iron running and useful for tasks around the acreage and small-scale farm. This do-it-yourself guide to user-scale maintenance and repairs contains 30 projects that will help you keep your tractor in top running order and in safe and convenient shape for everyday use.

This manual applies broadly to 1960s to 1980s utility (40 to 100 horsepower) tractors, both diesel and gasoline powered. However, all of the knowledge is applicable to both older and newer tractors that today's small-scale and lifestyle farmers may use. Where newer or older tractors will likely be different, the project points out what may be different and what to look for.

In addition to basic preventative maintenance, the book features projects that are organized in chapters by systems, such as electrical and lubrication. Each chapter begins with an overview of why and where the system is likely to need attention, and then contains specific projects dealing with parts of the system.

Each project describes the need for the maintenance task and its benefits, and then conveniently details the time, special tools, parts needed (both necessary and nice to have), costs, expected difficulty, and skills necessary to complete the project safely and effectively. Each project is completely illustrated with color photo sequences depicting the steps in the project described.

In the not-too-distant past, many young, hard-driving farm operators had a grandpa or other relative who took pride in still being able to make a contribution by taking good care of maintenance tasks on tractors and machinery. Along with that, many rural kids grew up absorbing the fundamental hands-on skills of maintaining and fixing farm equipment, so they could step in to fill grandpa's shoes as the years went on.

The world has changed and those days have passed. My hope is that the information in this book will help fill the gap that has been left, and that the new generation of small-scale and lifestyle farmers can benefit from the skills once taken for granted as always being there.

My sincere thanks to the people and companies who allowed me to photograph or work on the tractors and supplies used for illustration:

- Massey-Ferguson 165 and 285: Vera and Bill Mokoski, Treco Ranch
- White 2-75: Pat and Donna Durnin, CAMAS
- John Deere tractors: Agro Equipment, Ziehr Farms
- Ford 2000 Orchard Special: Tony Heuver, Eagle Lake Nurseries
- Kubota L3400: Landholder Small Farm Solutions
- AGCO tractor: Wenstrom Equipment
- McCormick-Deering W-6: Frank Rouse, Rattray Reclamation
- Various parts, tools, and supplies: Princess Auto

This book would not have been possible without these people and companies, and the trust they extended in allowing their tractors to be worked on by this determined (but still amateur) heavy-duty-equipment mechanic.

A big thank you also to the many farmers and tractor enthusiasts from across the continent who share their knowledge, concerns, and tips on the Yesterday's Tractor Internet forums (*www.ytmag.com*).

Protecting Your Land and Health

In the course of this work, you'll be draining various fluids, some of which will not be reused. Rather than dump them on the ground, find out where there are recycling facilities near you and take them there.

This is not just a "tree hugger" issue anymore. The day is approaching (and in some places, already here)

where an environmental audit will be required for any real estate transaction. If you have a yard that's polluted with all sorts of oil, leaking batteries, and so on, you could be faced with a major cleanup expense before you can sell your land. Who needs that? There are recycling facilities in many places nowadays, such as at dumps, bulk-oil suppliers, and fire stations. Making use of them is to your advantage.

In terms of health and safety, some of the items you'll be dealing with are potentially flammable, toxic, or damaging to your skin and eyes. Wear proper protection, keep flame sources well away from your work, and be safe. You may be behind schedule now, but think how much further you'd be behind with a broken finger or scalded eyes. Be safe, use the right tools and supplies, and you'll be able to take pride in what you can accomplish in these projects.

——Rick Kubik, Certified Crop Adviser
American Society of Agronomy

CHAPTER 1
TOOLS, TECHNIQUES, AND SUPPLIES

In the maintenance projects that follow, you'll find reference to some special tools and supplies, and the techniques you'll need for using them. Most are relatively inexpensive, easily available, and often useful for jobs besides tractor service.

However, you will also need a selection of basic shop tools. The ones you may have for maintaining on-road vehicles will do as a start, but with tractors you are in the realm of heavy-duty mechanics, so it's a good idea to get tools to match.

Note: while inch-measure tools are described by way of example, metric sockets and wrenches are needed for tractors that use metric fasteners.

Basic Tool Kit
- 1/2-inch-drive socket set, with sockets from 1/2 to 1 1/2 inches. The 1/2-inch-drive handles and sockets are all more robust than the 3/8-inch drive typically used for cars and light trucks.

- Set of combination (open-end and box-end) wrenches from 3/8 to 1 1/2 inches.
- Set of double-ended wrenches (e.g., 3/8 and 7/16 inch, 1/2 and 9/16 inch, and so on). These are handy when the bolt head must be held while the nut of the same size must be turned.
- Large ball-peen hammer (24 or 32 ounce).
- Soft mallet for loosening or driving things that must not be damaged by using a steel hammer. Double-faced soft mallets are available with a variety of face materials such as rubber, rawhide, hard plastic, or brass.
- Punches, including pin punches, for driving stubborn pins or bolts out of holes.
- Screwdrivers.
- Pliers.
- A 1/4-inch-drive socket set is also nice to have for use on small nuts and bolts in tight quarters, such as in instrument panels.

The big lads. This is a 1-inch-drive socket set, for sizes up to 3 1/8 inches and is about $120. You probably won't need to go quite this big (car keys are at the top for scale), unless you are working on steel-tracked tractors. A 1/2-inch set should do the job for most tractors. This set could however make a nice surprise gift for the person who thinks their shop has everything!

Basic Supplies

Along with the tools, you'll need basic shop supplies such as:

- Coveralls and eye protection.
- Fire extinguisher.
- Penetrating oil to loosen fasteners.
- Grease gun and extreme pressure (EP) grease. A pistol-grip grease gun with flexible hose is handy for both ordinary work and tight places. Cordless electric grease guns are also now available at reasonable prices.
- Pencil and paper (or camera) to make records of how things looked before they were taken apart.
- Rags or shop towels.
- Buckets or pans to catch draining fluids.
- Sawdust or other blotting material (e.g., shredded paper or cat litter) for oil and fuel spills.
- Funnel, preferably one with gauze filter.
- Measuring jug for oil, coolant, etc. Do not use household measuring containers, they're too small.
- Some type of pad (e.g., cardboard) for lying on while under the tractor.
- Solvent for cleaning parts. Do not use gasoline because the vapors it constantly gives off are extremely flammable. A solvent such as Varsol cleans just as well but has a higher "flash point" (is harder to ignite).
- Wooden blocks for blocking wheels.
- A strong jack and jack stands or large wooden blocks (cut-off logs are good) to support the tractor when lifted.
- Measuring tape.
- Hand-cleaning soap/oil.
- Pair of mechanic's gloves, which are handy for the really messy jobs, nice to have around, and help keep your fingers from getting banged up when working in tight quarters or handling big parts.

Torque Wrenches

Steel bolts may look tough, but it may surprise you to know that steel bolts are actually slightly elastic and stretch a measurable amount when tightened. That's why bolts in some critical applications (e.g., cylinder heads or wheel bolts) often have a specified tightening force. Too much or too little may cause some sort of expensive and/or dangerous component failure.

Bolt tightening is measured with a special wrench called a torque wrench. When the specified tightening force is reached, the wrench supplies some sort of indication such as a dial reading or a click. It's true that a torque wrench is something you may only use now and

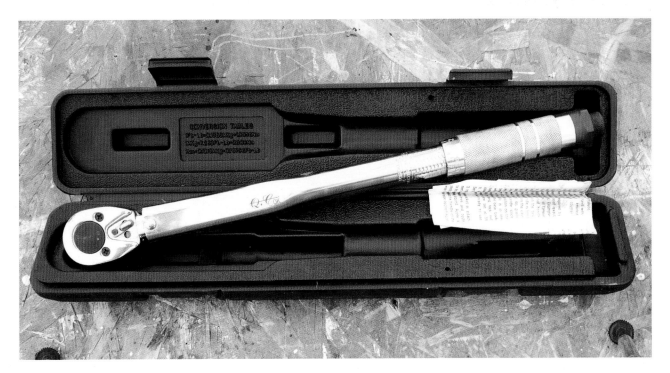

A click-type torque wrench with protective hard case. To save from having to rummage through the manual every time, make a card in the case that lists the tractor's key torque specifications and keep it with the torque wrench.

Head markings on bolts. Top row, from left to right: inch-sized ordinary steel (SAE Grade 5) and higher-strength Grade 7. Bottom row, from left to right: metric ordinary steel and Class 8.8 bolts. Bolts with no head markings can be assumed to be of lower strength. As bolt grade/class rises, the bolt receives heat treatments that make it stronger, but also more brittle.

then, but prices of torque wrenches have come down considerably in the last few years. Even a low-end torque wrench or using the backwoods method of "tighten it until you groan" is better than no torque wrench at all.

Ask your parts supplier about a good torque wrench size for use on your size of tractor (1/2-inch drive is probably the best). When you choose one, learn how to use it and recognize the sound/feel associated with click-type wrenches. Whatever torque wrench you choose, remember that it is a precision instrument and not one that should be allowed to knock about among the regular wrenches. Keep the torque wrench in its protective case and away from moisture.

Note these key points about torque values:
• They are based on the diameter of the shaft (threaded part of the bolt), not the bolt head size. For example, a 3/8-inch bolt has a shaft size of 3/8 inch, but a head size (across the flats) of 9/16 inch. If you try to twist that puppy to 120 foot-pounds (torque value for 9/16-inch bolt), you'll snap it right off before you ever get close.
• They apply to threads lubricated with oil or with locking compound applied. If anti-seize compound is used, reduce torque value by about 20 percent.

For bolts with no specified torque, general values can help prevent over- or under-tightening.

TYPICAL INCH-SIZE TORQUE REQUIREMENTS

Note: The values in the following chart apply to ordinary steel bolts commonly found on tractors (grade 5, rigid joints). For lower grades, reduce torque by 20 to 25 percent; for upper grades and other materials, see service manual.

Bolt diameter (inches)	Typical torque (foot-pounds)
1/4	9
5/16	17
3/8	33
7/16	52
1/2	80
9/16	120
5/8	162
3/4	285
7/8	425
1	638
1 1/8	850
1 1/4	1,200
1 3/8	1,550
1 1/2	2,075

TYPICAL METRIC TORQUE REQUIREMENTS

Note: The values in the following chart apply to ordinary steel bolts commonly found on tractors (grade 7, rigid joints). For lower grades, reduce torque by 20 to 25 percent; for upper grades and other materials, see service manual.

Bolt diameter (mm)	Newton-meters	Kilogram-centimeters	Kilogram-meters
5	4	40	-
6	7	70	-
8	17	170	-
10	30	300	3.0
12	53	-	5.3
14	86	-	8.6
16	135	-	13.5
20	275	-	27.5

CHAPTER 2
ELECTRICAL SYSTEM

Given that most tractors are diesels (which don't need electricity to ignite the fuel), it may be surprising that the biggest cause of breakdowns with both old and new tractors still involves electrical faults. It's mainly because connections in the electrical system are very susceptible to corrosion, heat, and vibration. These are generally small problems, ranging from hard starting to weak lighting, but they can still stop the tractor or make operation difficult.

The good news is that tractor owners can undertake several relatively simple maintenance projects to prevent and repair electrical faults. Electrical components, such as starters or alternators, have moving parts that fail or wear out, but the more common sources of problems are batteries that are low on water, corroded connectors in the wiring, or wire insulation worn away by rubbing against metal parts. The work is not physically hard, but it can sometimes take considerable patience and logical thinking to track down exactly where the problem lies.

Dude, Where's My Ground?

"Ground" or "earth" in the context of electrical systems refers to the path that current takes to get back to the battery. Rather than run return wires for every circuit, components are attached to the metal body and engine of the tractor and the metal acts as the common return path. That's why you'll see one terminal of the battery attached to the engine or frame.

Most tractors in North America since the 1950s will have a negative-ground system, and the following electrical system projects are written from that standpoint. If, however, you're dealing with older tractors and/or one from the U.K., it may use a positive-ground system (positive earth, as it's termed). Look for stickers near the battery and check which cable runs from the battery to the frame or engine block (ground). If you have such a system, to prevent system damage and sparking you'll have to substitute "negative" for "positive" and vice versa in all the electrical system projects.

The 24-volt systems have two 12-volt or four 6-volt batteries connected together in series. You need to reattach the cables exactly as they were before, so make a diagram of what goes where or put tags on the cables.

24-Volt Systems

While smaller tractors have the same kind of 12-volt electrical system found in cars, larger tractors have 24-volt systems. The advantage to a 24-volt system is that larger amounts of current can be run through the same size wires used in a 12-volt system. This lets the batteries provide greater amounts of power to starter motors that must crank large, hard-to-turn diesel engines.

Service procedures are the same for a 24-volt system, except for one crucial difference: if there is not a diagram in the battery compartment or manual, make a drawing so you know how to reconnect the cables.

Battery service tools. Each item costs about $5. Clockwise from center: wire brush for cleaning terminals, hydrometer, syringe for adding water, replacement positive terminal with anticorrosion washer, cable puller, replacement negative cable and washer, baking soda, and distilled water. Distilled water can be found in grocery stores. The hydrometer compares the specific gravity of the battery acid to plain water. The closer the battery is to fully charged, the higher the specific gravity, so the float rises higher. Battery and coolant hydrometers are not the same. Each must be used for its specific job.

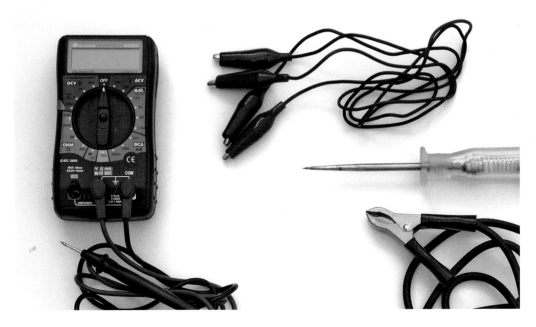

A digital multimeter with test lamp and LED charging system indicator with a hard case is about $20 at auto supply and hardware stores. The jumper wires (about $5 for a pack of four) can connect meter leads to terminals help free your hands during testing.

PROJECT 1 | Service Battery and Cables

Time: 1 hour

Frequency: Monthly

Tractor specs needed: None

Special tools: Battery service tools

Materials: Baking soda, distilled water, dielectric grease, several gallons of water for washing off spills

Cost: Very low

Skill level: Easy

Tip: The nuts on battery terminals tend to be heavily corroded and easily rounded off, so make sure you are using the correct size wrenches.

Maintenance Tip: One of the worst things for a battery is to sit unused for a long time, such as over winter. Batteries naturally suffer a gradual loss of power over time, and long periods of inactivity also cause a permanent reduction of battery power. If you know the tractor is going to sit for a long period, remove the battery and store it in a heated shop. Keep water levels topped and charge the battery once a month, and you'll extend its life by many years.

No matter what fuel your tractor runs on, it needs power from the battery to get started. While the tractor is running, the system charges the battery and maintains full power. This allows the battery to provide rated starting power, as well as the steady amounts of electrical power for lights, instruments, and other loads.

To take and hold a charge and to supply electrical power when needed, the battery needs to have the proper liquid level in its cells. During operation, chemical reactions in the battery cause water to be lost as gasses, slowly reducing the liquid level in each cell.

Caution: Always wear eye protection when servicing batteries. Batteries contain acid and accidental splashes of acid can burn your skin and eyes. Immediately wash the acid off with water to prevent burns.

When servicing batteries, it is wise to wear old clothes or coveralls because accidental contact with acid will eat holes in cloth. It doesn't show right away, but a day later your favorite pants may be full of holes.

1. Expose the battery or batteries enough so that the top is visible. This can be a chore in some tractors where large batteries are located in sometimes hard-to-access compartments. It's also why batteries often receive so little attention. Battery service is best performed with the battery out, but if it's a real wrestling match to get the batteries out, the service can be done in place.

Inspect the battery case for cracks or broken terminals that allow electrolytes to leak out. Batteries with cracked cases require replacement.

2. Before you remove any cables, make sure you can clearly identify the positive (+) and negative (-) battery terminals and cables (positive cables and terminals are generally colored red). Reinstalling the battery backwards is a surprisingly frequent cause of electrical system damage.

Expose the battery and check for any cracks or broken terminals.

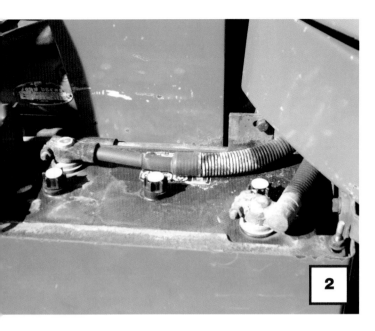

Check to make sure you can identify the positive and negative terminals and cables before you remove the battery or cables.

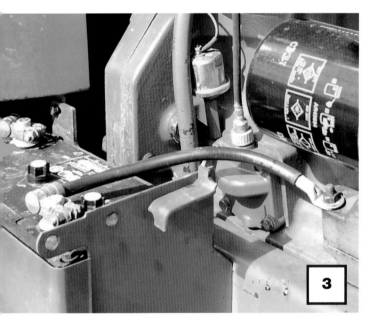

Remove the negative cable first and secure it so it doesn't touch the battery. Follow the same procedure with the positive cable.

side to side until it eventually loosens, or use the battery terminal puller.

Check that connectors are still securely attached to the cables. If they are, skip to step 5; otherwise continue.

4. If the cable-to-battery connectors are dodgy, new terminals can be attached to improve the connection and performance.

Remove the old terminals by undoing the bolts, if possible, or cutting with a chisel. Expose an area to be connected to the new terminals and remove any oxidation with a wire brush so that a good connection will be made. Clean any paint out of the connections areas of the new terminals and apply dielectric grease to prevent new corrosion. Use anti-seize on the clamping bolts of the new terminals so they don't corrode.

If you're dealing with a connector that has the cable and other wires molded in, just cut them off and attach the other wires with crimped ring connectors.

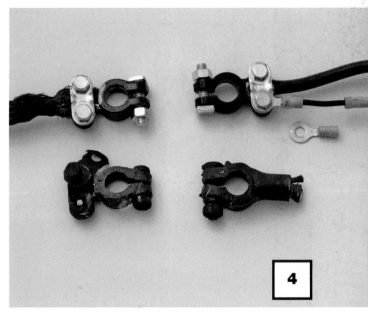

If the cable-to-battery connectors are in bad shape, replace the terminals for an improved connection and performance.

3. Detach the negative cable first and secure it so it cannot touch the battery. The ground cable is usually black and leads to the engine or frame as shown. After the negative cable is off, remove the positive cable and secure it to prevent accidental contact with the battery.

Don't pry off tight battery terminals—it will damage the battery. Instead, wiggle the terminal from

5. Wipe dirt off the top of the battery and clean corrosion off the terminals and case with a mixture of water and baking soda (three parts water to one part baking soda). Club soda can be substituted for the baking soda–water mix.

Use the wire brush to brighten battery terminals and connectors, and then apply a light coating of dielectric

This battery terminal is corroded.

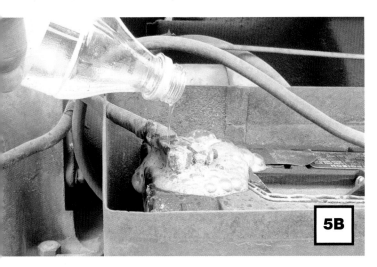

Clean off the corrosion with a water and baking soda mix.

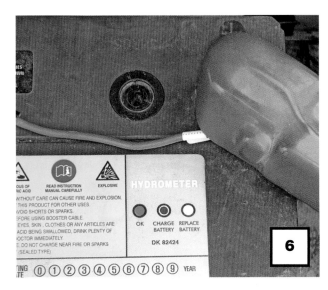

Examine the indicator eye if the battery is maintenance-free.

grease to slow further corrosion. Anticorrosion felt washers could also be added.

6. If the batteries are the maintenance-free type, all you need to do is examine the indicator eye.

Indicator display color	Battery condition
Green	OK
Black	Needs charging
White	Replace the battery

Examine the water level on refillable batteries.

7. On refillable batteries, examine the water level. Batteries with see-through cases should show the water level between indicator marks. On other batteries, unscrew the caps on each cell. The electrolyte level should be at the bottom of the split ring.

If any cells are low, top them with distilled water. Do not overfill and do not use tap water because it contains minerals that will ruin the battery.

8. For the measurement in this step, the surface charge of the battery needs to be removed, but don't worry, this

Specific Gravity	Percent of Charge
1.27	100
1.23	75
1.19	50
1.14	25
1.10	0

is easy. If the battery is out of the tractor, leave it for 24 hours in a warm place. If it is still in the tractor, reconnect it and turn on the headlights for a minute or two.

Once the surface charge has been removed, measure the state of charge with either the hydrometer or multimeter (digital meters only—analog meters are not sufficiently accurate).

Hydrometer test: For each cell, insert the hydrometer tip and squeeze the bulb to draw in enough electrolyte for a reading. If the hydrometer is marked with colored levels, the state of charge is shown directly. If the hydrometer is marked with numbers, refer to the specific gravity to the right.

Digital multimeter test: Touch the test leads to the battery terminals and read the voltage. For 24-volt systems, double the readings.

Percent of charge	Voltage
100	12.60+
75	12.40
50	12.20
25	12.00
0	below 12

If the battery is less than 75 percent charged, fully recharge it before proceeding. If the battery fails to take and hold a charge in 24 hours of charging, it should be replaced.

Replace the battery in the compartment and reattach any hold-down straps or clamps. Spray oil on the hold-down clamp threads to prevent corrosion. Reattach the positive battery cable first, then the negative cable.

9. A final voltage drop test makes sure there is a free flow of current between battery and cables, allowing full power from the battery to the starter and from the charging system back to the battery. Be absolutely sure the tractor is in neutral and the brakes are locked for this test because it requires that the engine be cranked. You don't want to be accidentally run over!

Place the multimeter test leads as shown: black touching the connector; red touching the battery post. Have an assistant briefly crank the engine without starting it, or use a remote starter switch. Do not short-circuit across the solenoid.

If the voltage reads 0.2 volts or more (0.6 volts on a generator system), there is resistance interfering with the flow of electricity. Clean the post and terminal and try again until the test is successful.

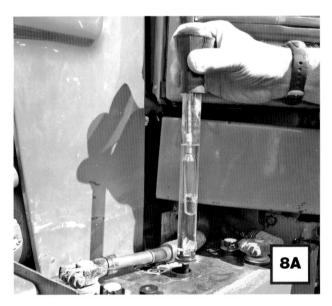

Insert the tip and squeeze the bulb to draw electrolytes into the hydrometer.

Connect the multimeter leads to the terminal to read the voltage.

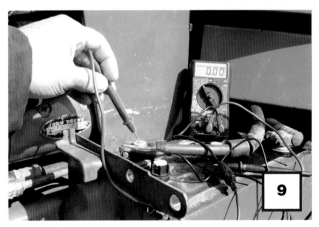

With the multimeter lead attached to the battery terminal and the cable end, have an assistant crank the engine without starting it to see if there is any resistance in the electricity flow.

PROJECT 2 | Test Charging Circuit

Time: 1–2 hours

Frequency: Annually, at start of season

Tractor specs needed: None

Special tools: Multimeter, jumper wires

Materials: None

Cost: None, unless components are replaced

Skill level: Moderate; requires recognition of parts

Tip: Practice using the multimeter for simple measurements, such as flashlight battery voltage, or resistance on various lengths of scrap wire.

Maintenance Tip: Once you've set the alternator drive belt tension to the correct specs, feel how it deflects when pushed by hand. In your checks before starting the tractor, you can then quickly feel if the belt is tight enough.

After the battery pours out power to the electric starter that cranks the engine to life, the engine's charging system puts energy slowly back into the battery to restore the charge. If you notice any of these symptoms on your tractor, it's a sign there are already problems in the charging system:

- When you turn the key to ON, the electrical-system indicator light does not light or the electrical-system gauge does not move.
- The battery is always losing water or the top is hot to the touch during operation.
- Headlights dim when the tractor idles.
- Some wire ends look "cooked;" wire insulation is blackened or brittle.
- Electrical ground connections show signs of corrosion.
- Alternator/generator drive belts squeal all the time.

The charging system is composed of not only the alternator or generator that produces current, but the battery that receives the current and the wires to carry it there.

If there's an old, poorly maintained battery in the system, its inability to accept the charge puts a tremendous strain on the other parts of the system. Strain in the form of heat destroys wiring and soldered connections in the alternator or generator. Similarly, if the wiring has high resistance and poor connections, the charge that is produced is turned into heat along the way and never makes it to the battery.

That's why before starting this project, you should perform battery maintenance project 1. Otherwise your efforts here may bear less fruit.

1. With the engine switched off and the key removed for safety, loosen the alternator or generator drive belt and examine its condition. Never simply pry the belt on

Loosen the alternator or generator drive belt and examine it for cracks, tears, or splits.

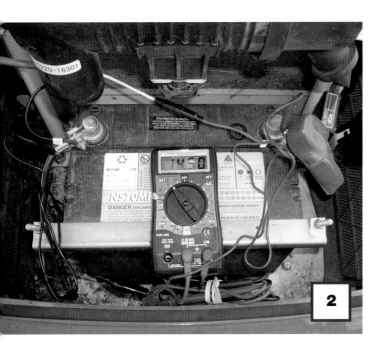

Measure the voltage being delivered to the battery with a multimeter.

stretched beyond the limits of adjustment and replace double belts in pairs.

2. Start the engine and run at high idle speed (greater than 1,000 rpm). Measure the voltage being delivered to the battery. Hold the red multimeter lead to the positive terminal of the battery, the black lead to the negative terminal, and the dial set to read DC volts.

Charging voltage should be 13.5 to 15.5 volts, which will keep the battery well charged. If it is above or below that range, further tests are needed. Note: For 24-volt systems, charging voltage is double that listed above; for 6-volt systems, half is listed.

3. If charge voltage is above 15.5 volts, there is a problem in the regulator, which will require testing and repair by a specialist. On newer tractors, the regulator is inside the alternator.

Older tractors may also have internal regulators or an external regulator, such as this one under the instrument panel of the Massey-Ferguson 165. External regulators can be removed and tested separately and replaced if necessary. Sometimes regulator problems are simply due to a bad ground. Clean the ground connection and retest.

and off because it will damage the belt and/or bearings in the alternator or generator.

Replace the belt if you see small cracks, greasy or glazed areas, tears, or splits. Small cracks will enlarge as the belt is flexed. Grease rots the rubber and makes the sides slick, which usually means the belt slips easily and makes a high-pitched squeal.

Spin the alternator or generator by hand. If it's hard to turn or there are loud grinding noises, there's a problem within the unit that will require diagnosis and repair by a specialist.

If the belt and alternator or generator seem okay, replace the belt and adjust it to the correct tension. If you don't have a manual listing belt tension specifications, you can do an approximate adjustment based on the length of belt between the alternator or generator pulley and the pulley that drives it.

Distance between pulleys	Belt deflection
Less than 12 inches	1/8 to 1/4 inch
12 inches or more	1/4 to 1/2 inch

A little too loose is better than too tight. A belt that is too tight will quickly wear out bearings in the alternator or generator, as well as any other component it drives, such as the coolant pump. Replace the belt if it is

There could be a problem with the regulator (located inside the alternator on newer tractors) if the voltage charge is above 15.5 or below 13.5 volts.

4. If charging voltage is below 13.5 volts, a quick-charging circuit test with the multimeter will tell if it's a problem with loose or corroded wiring between the battery and alternator or generator. Connect the multimeter as shown:

RED leads to the output terminal of the alternator or generator. The alternator output terminal is generally marked "BAT," while generator output terminals are generally marked "ARM."

BLACK leads to the positive (+) terminal of the battery. Jumper wires may be needed for making this length of connection.

Start the engine, turn on all electrical accessories (lights, cab fan, etc.), set throttle for engine rpm of about 1,500, and check the voltage.

If the above test shows the problem is in the wiring, the next project in this book describes what to do. If the wiring is okay, unbolt the alternator or generator (and external regulator if so equipped) and take them to a repair shop to be tested and rebuilt or replaced. Often you can trade in your old alternator or generator when you buy an already rebuilt one.

While removing the parts, make a lot of notes on how things fit together, which length of bolt and spacer goes where, and which terminals connect to what. Make simple diagrams or take pictures. The information will make reassembly much easier and prevent costly consultation on how to get it working again.

Alternator systems

Voltage 0.2 volts or less	Wiring is OK
Voltage more than 0.2	Problems in wiring

Generator systems

Voltage 0.6 volts or less	Wiring is OK
Voltage more than 0.6	Problems in wiring

There could be loose or corroded wiring if the multimeter reads lower than 13.5 volts.

PROJECT 3	Service Wiring

Time: 1–4 hours

Frequency: As needed

Tractor specs needed: Tractor wiring diagram is handy, but not essential

Special tools: Wiring tools

Materials: Electrical tape, dielectric grease, clips, grommets

Cost: Low

Skill level: Easy, but requires patience

Tip: If you've never attached new connectors before, practice crimping several connectors on scrap pieces of wire. The test for a good connection is simple: if you can easily pull it off, it's not good (a really hard pull will take a good connection off). Soldering can also be used to make a very solid mechanical connection. However, if continual breakage is a problem, consider routing wires so they are not under tension, and secure any lengths of loose wire with tape, zip ties, or insulated clamps.

Maintenance Tip: While you're doing other maintenance, such as oil changes or greasing, inspect any electrical system wiring in the area for broken wires, worn insulation, or corrosion on the connections.

Even if the tractor's battery, charging system, and starter are good, minor problems with wiring and connectors can be the downfall of the electrical system. Bad wiring is similar to leaky hoses or plugged taps in a lawn system: the power dribbles out along the way instead of getting to where it's needed.

Corrosion, heat, vibration, and age are the enemies that gradually degrade the efficiency of the wiring. A lot of the time electrical problems are nothing more than a bad ground or corroded terminal. Most can be quickly repaired when spotted before they become a tractor-stopping problem.

Tractor wiring comes in various gauge (thickness), depending on how much current it is expected to carry and how long the wire needs to be. The larger the number, the smaller the wire.

If replacing any sections of wire, use the same gauge. The color of the wire insulation makes circuit identification simpler. If you can't match the color, you can put a tag (written in weatherproof ink) on each end of the wire for foolproof identification in the future.

Look for broken or burnt electrical wires and make sure the connectors are secure.

ELECTRICAL-WIRE SIZE GUIDE
(for distance less than 6 feet)

12-volt current	Wire gauge
Up to 5 amps	18
Up to 10 amps	16
Up to 15 amps	14
Up to 20 amps	12
Up to 30 amps	10

You can add wire if the connector is too short and doesn't have enough slack.

1. Examine electrical wires for broken or burnt insulation. Pay special attention to anywhere the wire rubs against metal and might create a short circuit. Wiggle the connectors to make sure they are secure and the wire near them is not brittle. If there are any bad spots, wrap them in several layers of electrical tape. Try to spot the source of heat or wear and use a grommet or clip to move the wire away from the source to prevent further problems.

2. If a connector is loose or corroded, check that there is enough slack in the wire to remove the bad connector and attach a new one. If not, add a short length of wire with a butt connector, then attach the new connector to the piece of wire you've added.

In this case, the frayed section of wire was clipped off and a new ring connector (yellow) was crimped on to demonstrate the connection.

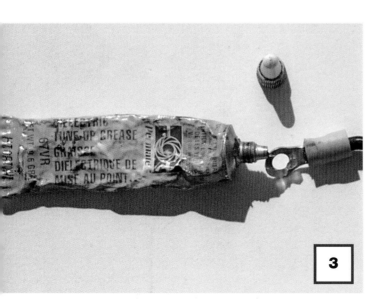

A light dab of dielectric grease on the connector will prevent corrosion.

3. When attaching connectors, apply a light dab of dielectric grease to prevent corrosion, but don't apply so much that it attracts dirt and makes subsequent work messy.

If a light is not working and the bulb and fuse look okay, there is a wiring problem either with a bad ground (most likely) or no power coming to the socket. With this socket, the problem was finally traced with a test lamp to a poor connection where the ground wire (black) was riveted to the metal light socket holder. As a solution, the ground wire was cut off and soldered directly to the socket to make a sure ground.

Over time, condensation and water can cause hidden corrosion in the metal parts of fusebox, which leads to strange intermittent electrical failures even though the fuses all are good. Brush away all corrosion and give the whole fusebox a thorough spraying with electrical contact cleaner.

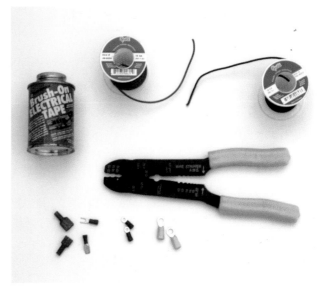

Wiring tools. The insulation color on crimp-on connectors matches the color of the top notches on the crimping pliers. Automotive-grade connectors are generally sufficient, but if moisture or mechanical loosening is a particular concern, buy marine-grade connectors at a boat supply house. The small notches between the handles of the crimping pliers allow you to strip insulation from the wire to prevent nicks in the wire that can happen when you use a knife to strip insulation. Tiny nicks in wire strands create a potential site for breakage and corrosion.

The so-called "scotch tap" connector allows you to easily connect to a wire that already carries current (e.g., the yellow one). Tape the connection thoroughly after splicing to prevent loosening and development of corrosion.

Heat-shrink tubing is available in a wide range of diameters and colors and provides an excellent way to protect and insulate electrical connections. Cut a suitable length of the tubing (located in this demonstration loop at the 12 o'clock position) over a wire connection (9 o'clock), then heat slightly with a match to make the tubing form a tight fit over the wiring (5 o'clock position).

Dielectric grease allows the passage of electricity, but it seals out air and moisture to prevent new corrosion from forming. Use a small amount on every electrical connection to ensure long service life and easy disconnection.

Grommets and insulated clips make a secure, neat job on wiring. The upper grommet has been cut in half to show how it fits in sheet metal. Use a grommet anytime a wire passes through a hole in thin metal so it does not saw through insulation and create a short circuit. Insulated clamps perform a similar function and keep lengths of wiring away from damaging heat, abrasion, or risk of tearing.

PROJECT 4 | Service Instruments

Time: 1/2–4 hours, depending on complexity

Frequency: As needed

Tractor specs needed: Wiring diagram is handy, but not essential

Special parts: Identified in the course of testing

Special tools: Electrical testing tools

Materials: Dielectric grease, electrical tape

Cost: Low if bulbs or loose wiring are the problem, higher if instruments or switches must be replaced. Instruments such as voltmeters, ammeters, or fuel gauges are about $20 each.

Skill level: Easy, but requires patience, logical thinking, and dexterity

Tip: This job can involve a lot of wire tracing in tight quarters under the instrument panel, so budget plenty of time for the job.

Maintenance Tip: If the gauge stays near "Full" for a long time and then seems to show a rapid movement to "Empty," try inserting inexpensive resistors in the line from the sender and observe how the readings change. One to 10 ohms may be all that's needed for a more accurate gauge.

Many older tractors have inoperative instruments that operators have grown accustomed to working without. If the tractor starts and runs, many assume warning lights aren't really needed and assure themselves that regular filling eliminates the need for a fuel gauge.

But did you know that if your red alternator light does not come on when you switch on the tractor, the charging system may not be working and the tractor could fail to start when you're miles away from help? Or if you accidentally run out of diesel fuel because the gauge isn't working, all the sediment in the bottom of the tank is sucked into the filters and leads to a messy and time-consuming filter change?

This project involves servicing two of the most important gauges/lights: charging system function and fuel level. The techniques for checking and repair can be applied to most other instruments on the tractor by finding and testing the senders, power supply, and ground connections.

Charging System Indicators

When you turn the key to ON, there should be some sort of indication on the instrument panel that the electrical system–warning indicator is working, either an indicator light coming on or some movement in the ammeter/voltmeter.

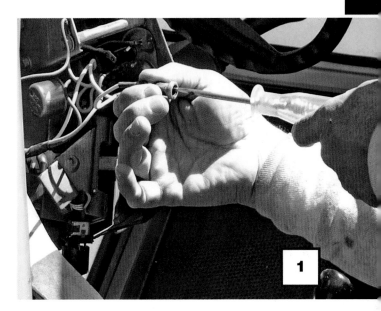

Bulbs are held in the instrument panel by a metal twist-in socket, rubber push-in holder, or by the lens that threads into the bulb socket.

1. If the red battery light does not come on when you turn the key to ON, but there's still enough cranking power to start the engine reliably, it often means a burnt-out bulb, so that's the first place to check. Bulbs are generally held in the instrument panel by a metal

25

twist-in socket, rubber push-in holder, or as in this case, by the red lens that threads into the bulb socket. The hardest part of this step can be getting at the bulb on the back of a tight instrument panel. It may mean the removal of the hood or instrument panel cover first.

If the bulb filament doesn't look burnt out, the bulb is probably good so the next thing to check is to see if there's corrosion or poor contact in the bulb socket. Use the test lamp with a good ground connection (right to the battery, if you like). Remember to switch the key to ON for this test.

If the test lamp lights, which indicates that power is coming in, the ground connection is probably bad (service is outlined in project 3). Check the bulb in the socket again at this point to confirm that it works.

If the test lamp does not light, use the wiring diagram or wire colors to trace the circuit and check with the test lamp along the way in order to find the break.

2. If your tractor is equipped with an ammeter or voltmeter and there is no sign of movement in the gauges, it's often a bad connection. Use a multimeter to check that the voltmeter or ammeter circuit is receiving current with the engine running and that the ground connection is good.

If the circuit is dead, find and repair the fault as outlined in project 3.

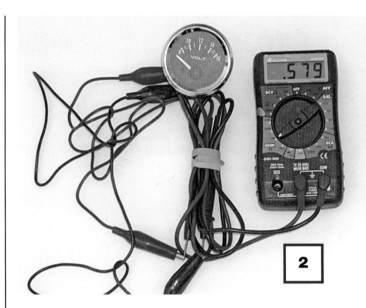

Reading the internal resistance of the gauge helps determine whether it is functional.

If the circuit is live, disconnect the wires to the meter and check the resistance of the meter itself. A functioning voltmeter should show several hundred ohms resistance and a functioning ammeter should show near-zero ohms.

Replacement ammeters and voltmeters are readily available from tractor supply dealers.

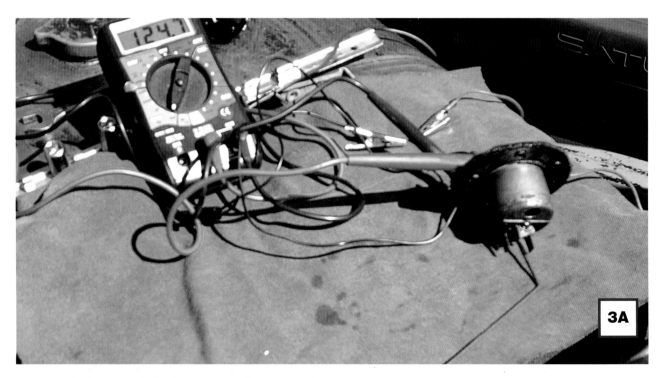

Check electrical resistance when the float is low (i.e. empty tank).

Check the electrical resistance when the float is high (i.e. full tank). There should be a clear difference. If not, the sender is not working properly.

3. The fuel gauge has three parts that can cause trouble: the sender unit in the tank, the gauge on the panel, and the wiring in between.

Caution: When testing the fuel tank circuit, do not apply voltage to the circuit. This will damage the sender or gauge and could cause an explosion in the tank.

The first place to check is that the wires are attached to the sending unit. Often these are broken off during repairs or become corroded over time. Brush off any corrosion, apply dielectric grease, and replace bad connectors (as outlined in project 3).

The sending unit inside the tank functions on the basis of varying electrical resistance as a float falls (3A) or rises (3B) with the fuel level. The sender has been removed in this example to illustrate differences, but it can be checked in place by emptying and filling the tank.

If the sender isn't working, it will need to be removed and replaced with a new unit. Clean any dirt or corrosion away from the unit first, then undo the retaining

bolts. Remove it slowly so that no pieces of gasket fall into the tank.

If the sending unit is fine, check the wiring. Use the multimeter to check that the resistance of each wire goes from the sender to the gauge or to the ground. The wiring diagram is handy but not essential for this identification. Inspection and wire tracing will eventually reveal the path. To help in identification, check the color of the wires going to the gauge. One should be the same color as one of the wires at the sending unit.

Resistance readings between wire ends should be near zero. If any are not, find the broken spot in the wire and repair it or bypass the broken wire with a length of new wire from the sender to the gauge. If the color of the new wire is not the same, attach a written tag to both ends to help with future service.

If the sending unit and wiring are okay, make sure the gauge is receiving power. With the key switch on, use a test lamp to confirm that current is being supplied from one of the wires that you can trace back to the battery or fusebox (hot wire). If there is no current being supplied (don't forget to turn the key on), the problem is often a corroded connection. Clean the connection and retest until a current is received at the gauge.

4. Now that you've tested all the wiring, the only problem left is the gauge itself. If it still doesn't work, buy a new gauge the same diameter as the old one. Fortunately, gauge sizes are fairly standard.

Install the gauge according to the instructions in the package and connect the wires. On this gauge, the correct place for the power, sender, and ground wires are cast right into the back of the gauge for error-proof hookup.

5. Certainty of fuel level has been once again achieved.

Install the gauge according to the instructions on the package and connect the wires.

The correct fuel level is now achieved through the new gauge.

PROJECT 5	Service Spark Plugs (Gasoline Engines)

Time: 1/2 hour

Frequency: Every 100 hours of engine operation

Tractor specs needed: Spark plug gap

Special tools: Spark plug socket, thin file, spark plug gapping tool

Materials: Anti-seize compound, masking tape, and pen for tagging wires

Cost: Low

Skill level: Moderately difficult

Tips: Be careful not to drop a spark plug on a hard surface. A substantial part of the plug is made of porcelain, and even a tiny crack means the end of its life.

The spark plugs on tractors fueled with gasoline, LPG, or propane need periodic servicing to make sure that they can deliver the hot sparks needed for efficient combustion. Before removing spark plug wires from spark plugs, use masking tape to make a tag to wrap around the wires. Number the spark plug wires in sequence from the front to the back of the engine so you can reattach them to the correct spark plug. It's not important to replace the spark plugs themselves in the same socket they came from, but it is vitally important that the spark plug wires be attached in the same order from the front to the back of the engine.

Unless you have owned the tractor since it was new, start by buying a set of new spark plugs of the right type for the engine. With a used machine, the previous owner may or may not have installed the correct spark plugs. You'll need new ones eventually, so have a set of the right ones on hand. Try to replace spark plugs as a set so they are all of the same age and condition.

Determine the correct spark plug gap, either from your manual or at the tractor supply dealer where you buy the plugs. Even new plugs should have the gap set and checked before installation. If the gap is too small, the spark will be weak; if the gap is too big, the plug may not spark at all.

1. Pull on the rubber cover (boot) to remove the wire. You may have to wiggle and twist it a bit. Do not pull on the wire itself because that will damage it.

Pull on the rubber cover to remove the wire.

Check the level of electrical resistance in each wire. They should alll be the same.

Unscrew the plugs with the spark plug socket.

Examine the tip of every spark plug.

2. Examine each wire for cracks in the insulation and check the level of electrical resistance. Wires on some tractors may have a built-in level of resistance to reduce radio frequency interference. Look for an "R" marked on the wire.

Replace the wires as a set if there is any doubt as to their condition. Rust and corrosion in the connectors can affect resistance readings dramatically. Jiggle the test leads to test. Replace the wires as a set if the readings vary much from wire to wire.

3. Using the spark plug socket, unscrew the plugs by turning counterclockwise. It should not take extraordinary force to loosen them. If the plug refuses to budge, spray some penetrating oil on it and let it sit to give it time to work into the threads.

4. As you remove each plug, examine the tip. Ideally they will be brown to light gray, indicating fuel mixture is set correctly.

Bend the plug's side electrode with the plug tool to make room for the file.

File both sides of the air gap to expose clean metal.

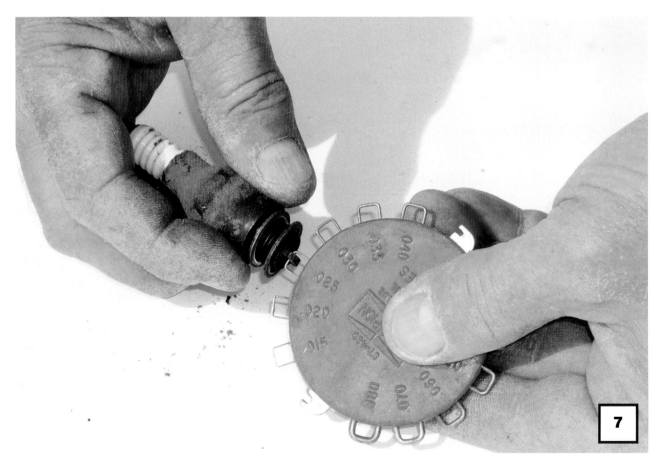

When the air gap is correct, a wire-type gauge will snap when it passes through the gap.

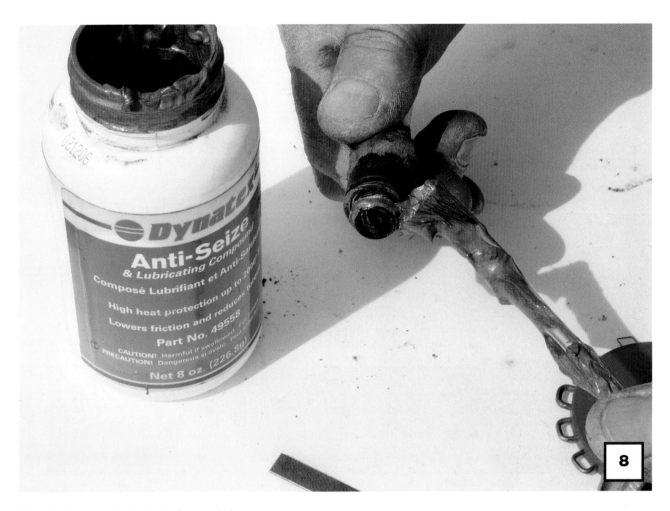

Dab anti-seize compound on the threads of each spark plug.

If any or all of them are oily, heavily crusted with deposits, or look like they've been striking metal, it's a pretty good sign that all is not well inside the engine. Take the plug, as is, to show to a tractor mechanic and discuss what may need to be done.

If all the tips are covered with dry black soot, it's a sign that the choke was on, the air filter needs cleaning (see project 10 or 11), or there are carburetor problems (see project 14). These plugs are probably still useable if the soot is brushed off.

If a tip looks wet and smells of fuel, there was no spark at that plug, so there's some further troubleshooting to be done. Do not reuse this plug until you've tried a new one to see if that cures the problem.

5. Use the wrench on the plug tool to slightly bend up the plug's side electrode to make room for the file.

6. Lightly file the surfaces on both sides of the air gap to expose clean metal.

7. Whether the plug is new or being reused, set the air gap to the correct distance by bending the side electrode up or down. When the gap is correctly set, a wire-type gauge of the right size will pass through the gap with a slight snap, similar to the sound and feel when dental floss passes between tight teeth.

8. Dab some anti-seize compound on the threads of each spark plug. Screw them in by hand, then tighten firmly (about 1/8 turn more) with the spark plug socket. Reattach the plug wires to the spark plug wires in the correct order.

This is a typical oil pressure sender unit for an electrically operated gauge. When oil pressure is low (e.g., when the engine is off or low on oil when running), the internal switch is closed so the warning light is switched on. When oil pressure is sufficient, the switch is open and turns the warning light off. On some diesel tractors, this may also control the current flow to the electrical system.

Indicator bulbs are pretty straightforward. If it comes on when you turn the key and goes out while the tractor is running, all is well.

Voltmeters measure volts (v) of electric charge in the system. When the key is switched on, the gauge should show about 12 volts. Once the engine starts, the gauge should show 13 to 14 volts are being supplied to recharge the battery.

Ammeters measure amperes (A) of current and whether that current is flowing out of the battery (-) or into it (+). When starting, the gauge should indicate a negative (-) current, then a positive (+) current once the engine is running and recharging the battery. If the engine starts but shows a discharge (-) while running, the battery is not being recharged.

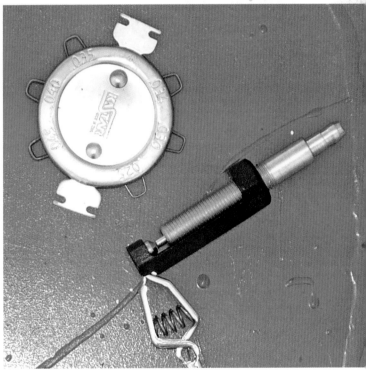

Spark plug sockets have a special rubber insert that grips the plug once it's unscrewed. This lets you easily lift the plug away from the engine, even if the plug is located in a deep recess in the cylinder head. The gap gauge has a small wrench to bend electrodes and round wire gauges to measure electrode gap.

This tool (about $10) allows a quick check of spark without removing the spark plug. Connect the spark plug wire, turn the screw in or out to adjust the spark plug gap, and clip the tester to the engine block. Cranking the engine will show if a spark is being produced or not.

The breaker points and condenser live inside the distributor, which has wires to send electricity in turn to each spark plug.

<table>
<tr><td>PROJECT 6</td><td>Service Ignition Points
(Gasoline Engines)</td></tr>
</table>

Time: 2 hours

Frequency: Every 100 hours of engine operation, or at start of season

Tractor specs needed: Points gap

Special parts: Points and condenser kit

Special tools: Small wrenches, feeler gauge, needle-nose pliers, thin file

Materials: Electrical-system cleaner spray

Cost: About $30 for the new points and condenser

Skill level: Medium

Tip: Use a magnetic screwdriver to remove and replace the small retaining screws. This prevents a lot of frustration of dropping small screws into hard-to-reach spaces.

Maintenance tip: Tractor parts suppliers have electronic ignition kits (about $50) to replace the mechanical ignition parts in almost any distributor. These kits are straightforward to install, improve engine efficiency, reduce exhaust emissions, and eliminate periodic service. This is a useful upgrade to consider when it's time for ignition point service.

Spark ignition engines (gasoline, LPG, and propane fuel) require some sort of switch to send current to the spark plugs at the right time so the engine runs properly. Since about 1980, most spark-ignition tractor engines have been fitted with solid-state electronics to do this job. Older spark-ignition tractors will have mechanical breaker points that need periodic service.

There are four potential areas of wear in mechanical breaker points that create the need for periodic service:

1. The electrical contacts that switch electricity on and off become pitted and corroded from carrying high current.

2. The movable arm of the ignition point has a small fiber block that rubs against high points (cams) on the shaft in the middle of the distributor.

3. The "rubbing block" gets shorter with wear. In engines used for a very long time, the cams themselves may also get worn down.

4. With time and vibration, the insulation may break down inside the condenser, preventing it from working effectively.

Before starting this project, obtain new ignition points and a condenser from your tractor parts supplier. The existing parts may still be serviceable, but you will need new ones eventually. And if your tractor is old enough to use breaker-point ignition, getting replacements may prove to be harder in the future.

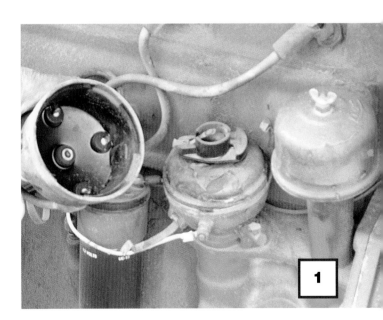

Make sure you can put the cap back on the distributor correctly before you fully remove the cap.

Pull the rotor straight up to remove.

Remove the dust shield to expose the breaker points.

1. Do not remove the spark plug wires. Undo the clips or screws that hold the distributor cap in place. Lift the cap up slightly and immediately set it back in place so you can feel how it fits back together. There will often be a groove or tab so the cap can only fit back on a certain way. Once you're certain you can reinstall it correctly, fully remove the cap.

2. Remove rotor by pulling straight up.

3. Lift off the dust shield to expose the old points and condenser.

4. Gently push the points open and examine the condition of the breaker points. If they can be cleaned up with a few strokes of a file and are meeting squarely, they can probably still be used and the condenser is also still useable. After filing the points, clean them with a shot of electrical contact cleaner spray and skip to step 9.

If the points are heavily worn or pitted (as shown), both the points and condenser need replacement so continue to step 5. As you remove the screws holding the old points and condenser, make notes or draw a diagram so you know how the new ones go back on.

Examine the condition of the breaker points.

5. Unbolt the lead from the condenser to the points, unscrew the condenser-retaining bolt, and remove the condenser.

6. Unscrew the points retaining bolt and remove the old points.

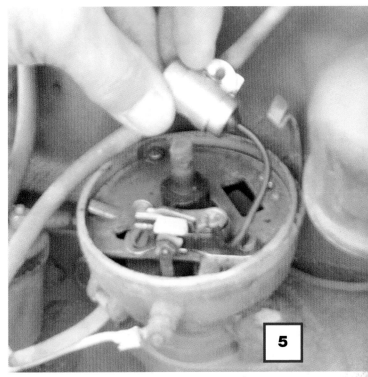

Remove the condenser.

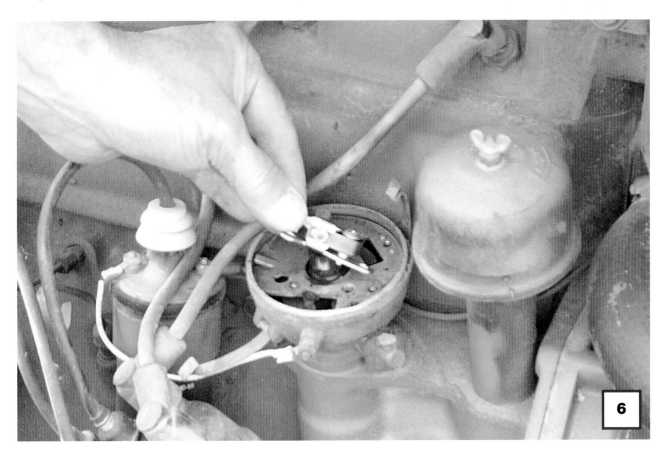

Remove the old points.

Clean the distributor camshaft and lubricate with grease.

Install new points and condenser.

7. Clean the distributor camshaft in the center of the distributor and lubricate it with the small vial of grease that came with the new points. The cams must be lubricated or the rubbing block will wear out rapidly.

8. Install the new points and condenser, taking care that the pin on the bottom of the points set fits into the hole in the mounting plate. Also be sure not to pinch or puncture the condenser. Needle-nose pliers are handy for getting the condenser lead in place.

Don't fully tighten the retaining screws just yet. You need to adjust the gap first.

9. Turn the engine so the rubbing block is on the high point of one of the cams. Using the feeler gauges, set the point gap to the specification for your tractor. Adjacent slots on the point assembly and the mounting plate allow you to partially insert a flat-blade screwdriver and gently open or close the gap.

Tighten the mounting screws and recheck the gap—it will probably have changed. Adjust and retighten until the gap stays within specs with the screws tightened. This may take some patience, but it's worthwhile. If the installed gap is too wide, the spark plugs won't get enough power, and if the gap is too narrow, the points will burn out quickly.

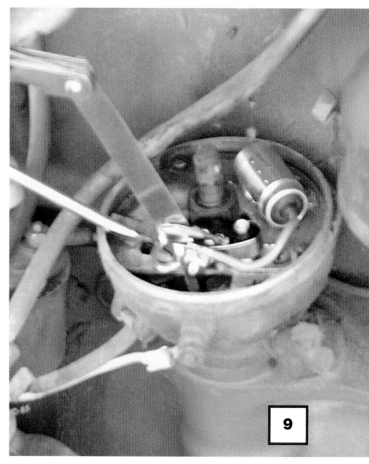

Set the point gap to the tractor's specification.

10

Reinstall the dust shield.

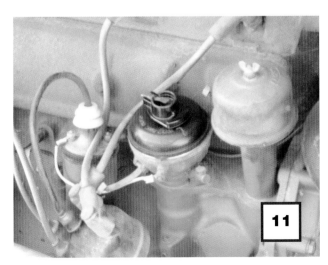

11

Install the new rotor.

10. Reinstall the dust shield. It may have a notch so it only fits in one position. In this case, the arrow points toward the distributor oil cup. If equipped with an oil cup, as in this example, put a few drops of oil in the cup.

11. Push on the new rotor. The flat spot inside the hole allows it to only fit one way.

Clean the inside of the distributor cap with electrical contact cleaner spray, wipe dry, and reinstall. Clean the top of the distributor cap and dry thoroughly between the terminals.

12. Clean and dry the top of the ignition coil (coil tower). If any part of the coil is cracked or leaking, replace the coil.

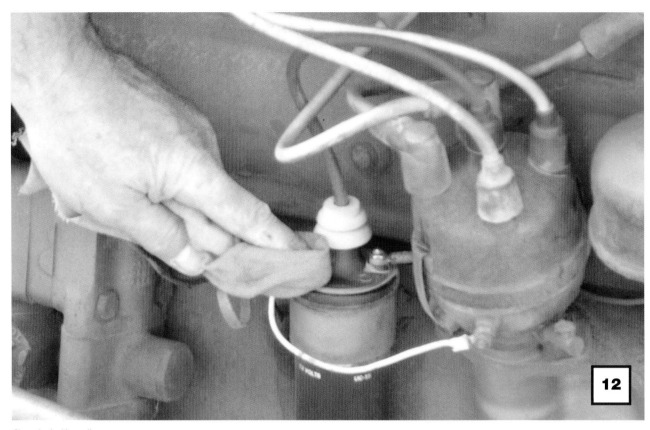

12

Clean the ignition coil.

This measuring tool is used to correctly set the gap between the components, such as clearance between cams and followers or electrical contacts on ignition points. The feeler gauge tool (about $10) consists of a number of metal "leaves" with their precise thickness marked on them. As you pull a leaf through a gap, you will feel a very slight drag if that gap equals the marked thickness.

The distributor tune-up kit for your tractor contains all the parts needed for this project: points, condenser, rotor, and cam grease.

CHAPTER 3
COOLING SYSTEM

Another common cause of tractor operating problems is overheating due to improper operation of the cooling system. Your tractor engine operates by converting fuel and air into heat, but much less than half of that heat goes into producing useful work. The rest of the heat must be carried away and transferred to the atmosphere, mostly by the cooling system.

Liquid in the cooling system circulates near the critical hot spots: exhaust ports, cylinder heads, piston bore sleeves, and so on. The coolant is then pumped into the radiator, where heat is efficiently transferred to the air. In rare cases, larger tractor engines are cooled directly with air, just like the small engines in lawn mowers or yard tractors. But most tractors over 18 horsepower are liquid cooled and will benefit from the projects in this section.

Before working on any liquid-cooled engine, let it cool down completely. Hot coolant or steam can cause severe burns.

Biting and stinging insects seem to have a great attraction to drained coolant, so to avoid attracting swarms of them, do these projects during cool morning temperatures or in a screened-in shop.

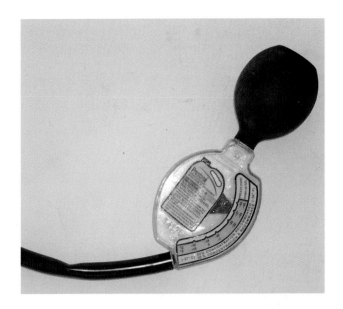

Most tractors use conventional green coolant, and the most common method for testing the coolant in the farm shop is with a coolant hydrometer, which checks specific gravity of the coolant. Other more precise and expensive tools (refractometers, test strips, etc.) are available if you prefer. Do not use your battery hydrometer for this check. It is a completely different tool.

In addition to maintaining the liquid part of a liquid-cooled engine, make sure the radiator is clear of debris, such as straw, insects, and dirt, so that air can flow freely over the fins to carry away heat. Check fan/alternator belt tension so that the cooling fan forces air through the radiator (see chapter 1, project 2, steps 1–2 for procedure).

Before you start this project, squeeze the upper and lower radiator hoses and inspect for weather damage (shown), cracks, tears, leaks, and loose or broken clamps. Hoses should feel firm and not show obvious bulges. If needed, obtain new hoses and clamps so you can replace them during the project while the cooling system is empty. It's so much easier to repair beforehand than having to fix hoses that blow during operation.

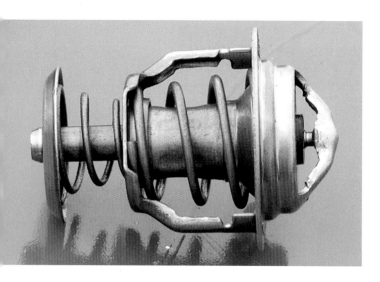

The thermostat is a heat-activated valve located inside the cooling system between the engine and radiator. When the coolant is cold, the thermostat is closed and keeps the coolant circulating only inside the engine block. This allows the coolant to quickly rise to the running temperature. When the coolant is hot enough, the thermostat opens and allows the hot coolant to flow into the radiator and lose excess heat.

Use a funnel with a filter to refill the system. Even though a clean bucket was used, this close-up of the funnel filter shows what was caught when refilling.

PROJECT 7	Test Coolant Concentration

Time: 15 minutes

Frequency: At least twice a year, preferably spring and fall

Tractor specs needed: Mark indicating proper coolant level

Special tools: Coolant hydrometer

Materials: Coolant, distilled water, rubber gloves, eye protection

Cost: Low

Skill level: Easy

Tip: To get a correct reading, no bubbles can remain attached to the float. Tap the hydrometer lightly to dislodge air bubbles.

Maintenance tip: Check coolant level and color whenever starting a heavy-duty engine, such as the one in your tractor.

The recommended coolant concentration in most engines is a 50/50 mix of coolant with distilled water. Maximum acceptable coolant system concentration is 60 percent in extreme cold, while the minimum concentration is 40 percent.

If coolant concentration is too high, the silicates will separate out of the coolant and form a paste that can plug radiators, create damaging hot spots in the engine block, and lead to coolant pump failure.

Remove the radiator cap and examine for coolant color.

If coolant concentration is too low, cooling system components can rust and corrode, hot spots from scale buildup can cause piston damage, and in cold climates there is the risk of cracked blocks from freezing.

A hydrometer cannot be used for measuring "long life" propylene glycol coolant/antifreeze solutions (red or orange in color) because specific gravity of this type of coolant does not vary consistently with concentration. This type of coolant is only found in relatively new tractors, so always refer to your manual for correct testing instructions.

All coolants are toxic to some extent and must be disposed of or recycled properly. The ethylene glycol in green coolants has a sweet taste, and ingestion by people, pets, and other animals has toxic consequences.

1. Let the engine cool down completely—overnight is best. Remove the radiator cap, or if your tractor is equipped with a coolant overflow tank, remove the overflow tank cap.

Examine the underside of the radiator cap for coolant color. It should be similar to the color of clean new coolant (i.e., green, yellow, or red). In this case, the color indicates that oil has somehow gotten into the coolant and formed a milky emulsion. This could indicate a leaking cylinder head gasket.

Also look at the cap for signs of rust or damage, and replace if its condition is doubtful. A tractor shop can pressure-test the cap, but a new cap is cheap insurance.

Inspect the inside of the radiator and wipe a fingertip underneath the opening as far as you can reach, checking for rust or corrosion that wipes off on your finger.

2. Insert the hose of the hydrometer into the coolant and squeeze the bulb to draw up sufficient coolant for a reading. Tap the case lightly to ensure no bubbles cling to the float. Read the coolant concentration on the hydrometer. Add coolant or distilled water to bring concentration within recommended levels: 50 percent is preferred, up to 60 percent for extreme cold, and no less than 40 percent.

3. Look down the radiator cap hole to inspect the core. It should look more or less like this almost-new radiator core. If you see a core with a lot of mineral scale buildup or a milky whitish emulsion (indicating oil in the coolant), consult a tractor mechanic as soon as possible.

4. Make sure the radiator or overflow tank is filled to the proper level. In this case, the level check shows coolant is up to the specified level. It also showed the coolant in the core is not nearly as milky as the coolant under the cap seen in step 3. This could indicate that the problem in the cap is due to oil somehow getting in around the cap. Securely replace the radiator and overflow tank caps.

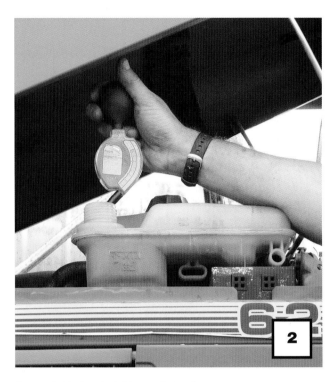

Use a coolant hydrometer to take a coolant reading.

Inspect the radiator core.

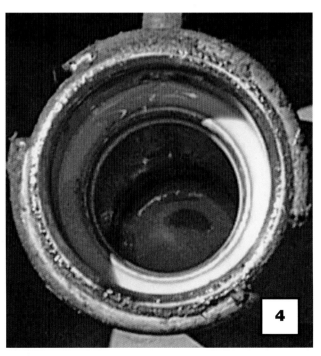

Make sure the radiator tank is filled to the proper level.

PROJECT 8 | Flush and Replace Coolant

Time: 2–3 hours

Frequency: Every two years

Tractor specs needed: Cooling system capacity, any special refill procedures

Special tools: Coolant hydrometer

Materials: Pan to catch old coolant, clean water for rinsing system (tap water is fine), jugs of fresh coolant, new or tested radiator cap, distilled water, tractor manual for information on the total amount of coolant in the system

Cost: Approximately $35

Skill level: Easy

Tip: Using chemical flush additives may or may not be useful or necessary. Ask your tractor parts supplier for a recommendation on what product to use.

Maintenance tip: The radiator cap is a low-cost item that should be considered a wear part. Every two years, either change it or have it tested at a radiator shop to make sure it can maintain the correct pressure in the cooling system.

Engine antifreeze does much more than keep your engine at its correct operating temperature by carrying excess heat to the radiator. One of the technical advances that made lightweight, high-powered engines possible was the development of modern coolants to run at high pressure. The radiator cap is a key part of the system because it keeps the system under higher than atmospheric pressure, which keeps the coolant from boiling away: higher system pressure = higher liquid boiling point = liquid that can carry more heat = more efficient dissipation of excess engine heat.

Coolant also lubricates and protects the cooling system parts such as cylinder bore liners and the coolant pump. Pure water does not have any pump lubricant or rust preventative. It is not a good idea to run an engine with only water as a coolant, even in a hot climate where protection against freezing is not needed.

There are three basic types of coolant:

Ethylene glycol (EG), or conventional coolant, is typically green.

Long life, or extended life, ethylene glycol is typically yellow.

Propylene glycol (PG) is typically red/orange.

Do not mix up these different types of coolant. Find the right type for your engine and add only that type blended with the correct proportion of distilled water.

Dilute antifreeze to the correct concentration (typically 50/50) with distilled water. Pure antifreeze is too thick for the engine to pump. Refer to the chart on the coolant jug for instructions on mixing to the desired concentration.

Tap water is not suitable for mixing because it contains dissolved minerals that will eventually cause expensive and unnecessary damage to engine parts. However, tap water can be used for flushing the cooling system.

Coolant breaks down over time, and its lubricating and cooling additives become less effective. The coolant should be drained and replaced every two years or longer in the case of "extended life coolants."

Check before you start with your tractor parts supplier or in the tractor service manual on the procedure for refilling the engine with coolant. On most engines, it's simply a case of pouring it in. But on some engines, it may be necessary to loosen the upper radiator hose and "burp" air out of the line until only coolant flows. If an air bubble remains trapped inside the cooling system, it will not function properly and the engine will overheat.

1. For safety and working comfort, let the engine cool down completely—overnight is best. Press down and turn to remove the radiator cap, and if your tractor is equipped with a coolant overflow tank, remove overflow tank cap.

Press down and turn to remove the radiator cap after the engine is completely cool.

Find the radiator's coolant drain point and drain the coolant.

Check for any drains on the engine block.

2. Locate the coolant drain point (tap or plug) on the radiator.

3. Many tractors also have a drain on the block. On bigger tractors they are easy to find, but on smaller tractors where things are tighter, they may be tucked in behind other components (e.g., just forward of the starter on the blue tractor).

The block drain is just ahead of the starter on this tractor.

4. Let all the coolant drain out completely and store it in a safely covered container until it can be recycled or safely disposed. With the drain points still open, run clean water into the highest point of the cooling system and let it drain out until it runs clear.

If you're going to replace any parts in the cooling system, such as hoses or the thermostat (see project 9), doing it while the system is empty will save time and bother.

5. Close all the drain points and add mixed coolant to the bottom of the radiator neck or other level indicated.

With the radiator cap still off, start the engine and run it for three minutes to circulate coolant through the engine and purge air bubbles. Check the level again and add mixed coolant as necessary. Replace the radiator cap and tighten it securely.

Drain the coolant and store in a secure and covered container until it can be safely disposed of.

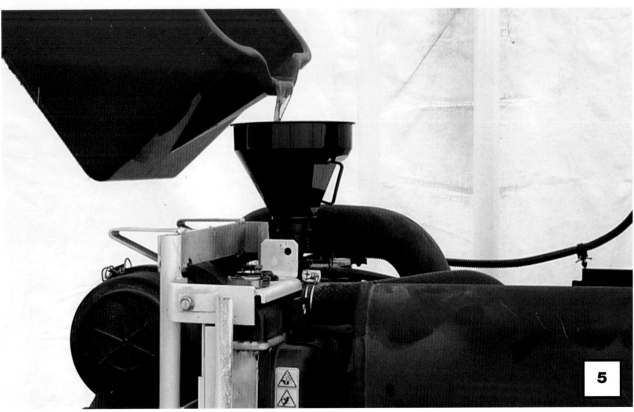

Close drain points and add new coolant.

| **PROJECT 9** | Replace Thermostat |

Time: 1–2 hours (less if done with coolant change/flush)

Frequency: Every 1,500–2,000 hours of engine operation

Tractor specs needed: None

Special parts: New thermostat and gasket

Special tools: None

Materials: Large pan to catch coolant, funnel with filter to refill

Cost: Generally under $50

Skill level: Medium

Tip: If the coolant that was drained out is being reused, strain it through a filter or cloth to remove any contamination.

Maintenance tip: To check for thermostat operation, feel the upper radiator hose as the engine warms up. You will feel a sudden gush of warm coolant start to flow through the hose if the thermostat is working.

Thermostats do not last forever—1,500 to 2,000 engine hours is a typical expected life. When they fail, they usually fail in the closed position and close off circulation to the radiator. Since this leads to overheating and sometimes blown gaskets or worse, periodic thermostat service is needed. Occasionally a thermostat may fail in the open position. In this case, the engine will take forever to warm up and run at a very low operating temperature, leading to poor fuel efficiency and increased exhaust emissions. Either way, periodic thermostat replacement or testing is a service project that can prevent a lot of downtime and engine strain.

If you have detailed engine operating specifications from your service manual or if the opening temperature is stamped somewhere on the thermostat, you can test the thermostat. Place a pan full of cool water on the stove with the thermostat fully covered by water. Use a thermometer to monitor water temperature. When the water temperature reaches the thermostat opening temperature, the thermostat should open in the center.

Check with your tractor parts supplier or in the tractor service manual on the procedure for refilling the engine with coolant. On most engines, it's simply a case of pouring it in. But on some engines, it may be necessary to loosen the upper radiator hose and "burp" air out of the line until only coolant flows. If an air bubble remains trapped inside the cooling system, it will not function properly and the engine will overheat.

1. For safety and working comfort, let the engine cool down completely—overnight is best. Press down and turn to remove the radiator cap, and if your tractor is equipped with a coolant overflow tank, remove the overflow tank cap.

CAUTION
HOT PRESSURIZED SYSTEM TO PREVENT BURN INJURY, REMOVE CAP SLOWLY.

1

After the engine is completely cool, press down and turn to remove the radiator cap.

2A

If the tractor has a drain on the block, too, you may only need to drain from there rather than empty the entire system.

2B

2. Locate the coolant drain points. All tractors will have a drain on the radiator; this tractor was drained from there. Let the coolant drain out completely and store it in a safely covered container until it's reused or can be safely disposed.

If your tractor has a drain plug on the block as well, you may only need to drain from there instead of emptying the entire system. On bigger tractors, block drains are easy to find, but on smaller tractors where things are tighter, they may be tucked in behind other components (e.g., just forward of the starter on the blue tractor).

2C

Some block drains can be hard to find and may be tucked behind other components.

3. The thermostat is usually located in a metal housing attached to the upper radiator hose. Unbolt the housing and see if it moves freely. You may need to remove the radiator hose as well. You may also need to tap the housing lightly with a wooden block to break it loose, as the gasket often sticks hard to the housing and engine block.

4. Remove the old gasket and take a good long look at how the thermostat fits. Compare it to your new one so you know how it goes back in, then remove the old thermostat. Stuff a rag in the hole to prevent anything from falling into the cooling system passages.

The thermostat is usually in a metal housing that is attached to the upper radiator hose.

Remove the gasket and remember how the thermostat fits.

Remove all traces of the old gasket.

6

Remove the rag and replace with the new thermostat.

5. Using a gasket scraper, remove all traces of the old gasket. Be careful not to gouge or scrape the metal, especially if the housing or engine block is aluminum.

6. Remove the rag you had stuffed in the thermostat hole in step 4. Place the new or tested thermostat in position.

7. Put the new gasket in place.

7

Install the new gasket.

8. Inspect the bolts before replacing the housing. In this case, the bolt on the right is starting to show whitish galvanic corrosion, which is common where steel bolts thread into an aluminum block. Brush off any corrosion and dab some anti-seize on the threads. Loosely bolt the housing back in place, then tighten the bolts evenly. If you previously removed the radiator hose in step 4, reattach the hose and tighten the clamp.

9. Close all coolant drains and replace the coolant. Add additional mixed coolant if needed, up to the bottom of the radiator neck or other level indicated.

With the radiator cap still off, start the engine and run it for three minutes to circulate coolant through the engine and purge air bubbles. Check the level again and add mixed coolant as necessary. Replace the radiator cap and tighten it securely.

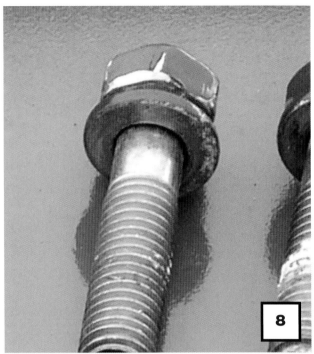

8

If there is any corrosion on the bolts, brush it off and dab some anti-seize on the bolt.

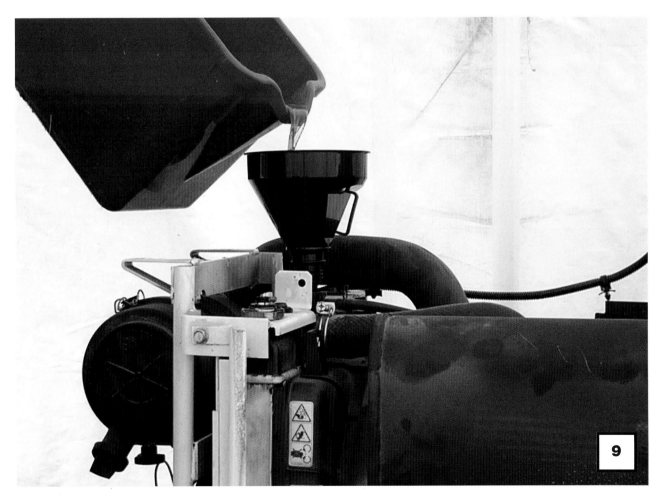

9

Close all drains and add new coolant.

CHAPTER 4
INTAKE AND EXHAUST

Tractor engines function like a large air pump. A typical tractor diesel engine, for example, requires about 8,000 gallons of clean air for every gallon of fuel consumed. That same volume of air must move out of the engine as exhaust.

Maintaining the intake air filter is easy, yet it is a much-neglected tractor service project. Plugged air filters result in hard starting, reduced power, increased exhaust smoke and air pollution, rough running, and increased engine wear. Intake air contamination problems can be caused by dirt falling into the air intake while changing the filter. Always turn the engine off when servicing the air filter, and cover the air intake while it's being serviced to prevent entry of dust, insects, and other contaminants.

Tractors are expected to operate under dusty conditions, so they almost always have some type of precleaner in addition to the main air filter. By removing large dirt particles before they reach the filter, precleaners extend filter service intervals and increase engine life.

Along with plenty of clean air, your engine also needs clean fuel to combine with air in a combustible mixture. Maintaining the fuel filters and occasionally the fuel tank keeps this part of the intake system in top condition.

Maintaining the muffler and exhaust pipes is equally necessary, though much less frequently needed. The engine designers chose the length of the exhaust pipes and type of muffler to achieve exhaust flow characteristics that contribute to efficient operation. Exhaust systems that are rusted out, broken off, or leaking will detract from engine performance and cause noise problems.

Above and right: *Some precleaners are simple screens, but better ones make the incoming air stream spin so dust and heavy particles fall out of the air stream and into the jar or bowl. Empty the receptacle frequently. If the plastic bowl has become so discolored that it is hard to see the dust level, replacements are available at tractor supply outlets.*

PROJECT 10 | Service Dry Element Air Filter

Time: 15 minutes

Frequency: Daily under regular use; monthly in occasional use

Tractor specs needed: None

Special parts: None

Special tools: None

Materials: Compressed air

Cost: None for basic service

Skill level: Very easy

Tip: Replace the filter with a new one after five to six cleanings, or once every two years, whichever comes first.

Maintenance tip: As part of the air filter service, also inspect the airflow path from the filter to the engine. Look for any indications that unfiltered air might be able to enter the engine. An unusual amount of dirt gathered at a connector could indicate a leak and allow unfiltered air into the engine. Tighten any loose clamps or bolts and replace or repair any sections of rubber connectors that are cracked.

Newer tractors are usually equipped with a dry element filter that is easy to install and service. Pleated sheets of resin-impregnated, heat-cured dry filter material trap and hold dust. The filter can be quickly and easily cleaned and replaced several times before a replacement filter is needed. Servicing the filter does however involve a lot of dust, so wear a dust mask if you are sensitive to airborne pollutants.

The rubber evacuator valve precleaner used on dry element filters allows the continuous ejection of dirt and water. Squeeze the rubber valve periodically to ensure that it is not clogged or that paint has not reduced the flexibility of the valve lips.

This item, usually found somewhere near the fuel filter, is an ether injector to aid in cold-weather starting.

Loosen the filter case clamp.

1. Loosen the clamp that holds the filter case together. If the case has a separate end cap, you'll also need to remove the thumbscrew in the middle of the filter.

2. Pull the filter out of its case.

Remove the filter.

Check rubber gaskets and thumbscrew for wear and damage.

3. Inspect the rubber gasket on the filter. Cracked, torn, or damaged gaskets are a major cause of intake air contamination. Also inspect the gasket on the thumbscrew (if so equipped). Replace the filter and/or thumbscrew if the gasket is damaged.

Check the inside of the filter for any signs of dirt. A dirty spot on the inside of the filter usually means that the filter is leaking and needs to be replaced.

4. Using compressed air, blow the filter clean from the inside out. You may need to tap the filter a few times on a wooden block or bench to loosen the dirt in the filter so it can be blown out. Insert the light into the filter and examine the filter outer surface. Any breaks in the filter will allow light to shine through, indicating that the filter must be replaced.

Once the filter is clean, put it back in the case, hand tighten the retaining bolt (if so equipped), and close up the housing securely.

5. Many tractors are equipped with a second, inner, dry-element filter. Service the same way as the outer filter. Service will not be required as often—refer to manual.

Use compressed air to clean the filter from the inside out.

Service inner dry-element filters just as you would service an outer filter.

<table>
<tr><td><h1>PROJECT 11</h1></td><td><h2>Service Oil Bath Air Filter</h2></td></tr>
</table>

Time: 1/2–1 hour

Frequency: Daily under regular use; monthly in occasional use

Tractor specs needed: Oil bath, oil viscosity

Special parts: None

Special tools: None

Tools: Parts-cleaning brush

Materials: Solvent for cleaning, solvent pan, correct viscosity oil for refilling

Cost: None

Skill level: Very easy, but messy

Basic service: Every 10–50 engine hours

Complete service: 1–2 times per operating season

Tip: Using the correct oil viscosity is crucial to proper oil bath–filter operation. Generally, the oil used is the same as recommended engine oil, but check for information on the filter body or in the manual. Incorrect oil viscosity will cause reduced power and white or blue smoke from diesel engine exhausts or black smoke from gas engine exhausts.

Maintenance tip: As part of the air filter service, also inspect the airflow path from the filter to the engine. Look for any indications that unfiltered air might be able to enter the engine. An unusual amount of dirt gathered at a connector could indicate a leak allowing unfiltered air into the engine. Tighten any loose clamps or bolts and replace or repair any sections of rubber connector that are cracked.

Incoming air comes down one passage of the filter and up another to the engine. As the dirty air makes a 180-degree turn at the bottom, it passes over a pool of oil. Dust and other particles are too heavy to make the turn, so they hit the surface of the oil and become trapped. Additional dust is trapped as it passes through the oiled mesh located above the oil cup.

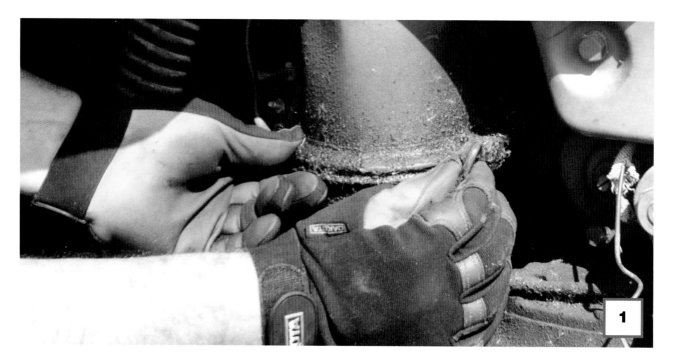

Unscrew the oil cup clamp.

Older tractors are often equipped with an oil bath filter. This type of filter is very effective and serviceable at low cost for the life of the machine. However, they do take longer to install at the factory (increasing build cost) and service in the field (increasing service cost).

1. Unscrew the clamp that holds the oil cup.

2. Pull the oil reservoir straight down and do not tip the container—it's filled with some nasty stuff.

Pull straight down to remove the oil reservoir.

Empty the oil reservoir and scrape out any sediment.

Fill the oil reservoir with fresh oil.

3. Empty the used oil and scrape out any sludge at the bottom of the reservoir. Clean reservoir with solvent and dry thoroughly.

4. Fill the oil reservoir to the correct level with the correct viscosity of oil. The correct level is stamped into the metal of the cup. Be sure to also replace the pan (at left in the photo above) in the cup. If you accidentally overfill the cup, just spoon the excess back out.

Reattach the oil resevoir and make sure it fits securely.

5. Reattach the reservoir to the filter and make sure it fits securely. Warped or dented reservoirs will not seal properly and must be replaced or repaired. If you've recently acquired the tractor and cannot be sure when the filter was last serviced, you should also clean the oiled mesh part within the filter.

In some filters this part can be removed and cleaned separately. On many other models the mesh is a permanent part of the filter housing above the removable cup, and the whole filter housing must be removed to service the mesh.

Soak the mesh in solvent and allow to dry. Dip mesh in correct viscosity oil and drain the excess. Reassemble and replace filter.

PROJECT 12 | Flush Fuel Tank

Time: 2–3 hours

Frequency: As needed

Tractor specs needed: May need fuel-injection-system bleeding procedure

Special parts: None

Specifications needed: None

Special tools: None

Materials: Fuel container, funnel, solvent, rags

Cost: None

Skill level: Easy in terms of skills, but the fuel tank and tractor body parts (e.g., the hood) can be heavy and awkward to handle.

Tip: For diesel engines, you may need to bleed air out of the fuel lines after doing this procedure. This information is found in the manual, so have it handy or find out the correct procedure from a tractor mechanic or parts supplier.

Maintenance tip: When letting the tractor stand for any length of time, especially in the off-season, fill the fuel tank as full as possible. This minimizes the space that can rust in metal tanks. It also provides time for water and contaminants to settle to the bottom of the tank where they can be drained out via the sediment trap.

A commonly heard problem on older machines is that the tractor starts and runs well for a while, but then it seems to suffer fuel starvation even though the filters have been changed and the tank is full.

This vexing problem is often related to an accumulation of dirt, rust flakes, and other contamination in the bottom of the tank. One service project found dead moths clogging the fuel outlet in a diesel tractor. The insects were apparently attracted to the fuel odors from the farm fuel storage tank, died inside the fuel hose nozzle, and then were pumped into the tank along with the fuel.

Another problem that took some time to solve involved disappearing accumulation in a tank. The tank had a small vertical pipe on the outlet so that fuel was never taken from the potentially dirty bottom of the tank. The engine kept dying from fuel starvation, but would start up fine after it sat idle for a while—the first two times it ran long enough to replace the fuel filters.

After much head-scratching, it was determined that dirt and rust flakes were being slowly pulled toward the outlet by fuel pump suction, piled up at the outlet, and blocked the flow. When the engine died, the suction stopped and the pile of contamination slumped back down, which left the outlet pipe clear again. The cycle repeated just when we thought things were sorted out.

Remove anything that blocks access to the tank.

The eventual solution was another thorough cleaning of the tank, as outlined in this project.

1. Remove any sheet metal that blocks access to the tank, such as the tractor hood.

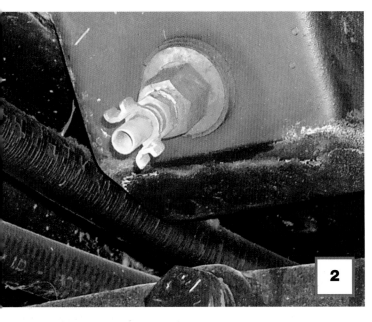

Find the fuel tap and let the tank drain completely.

2. Drain the tank completely. Because the fuel toward the bottom of the tank may be quite dirty, strain it through a clean cloth or other suitable filter if you are going to reuse the fuel.

This tractor has a convenient sediment trap at the bottom of the tank, which provides a way to drain the tank of water and contaminants daily—or you can drain the whole tank if you leave it open. Other tractors require disconnection of the fuel supply line to drain.

Don't drain the tank by letting the engine use all the gas because a lot of bottom-dwelling crud will get sucked into the fuel filters, and then you'll have to change them, too.

Once the tank is drained, disconnect any hoses connected to it. Diesel engines will also have a fuel return line that runs from the injection pump back to the tank, as well as the supply line that carries fuel to the engine.

Disconnect fuel-gauge sender wires. If your fuel gauge is not working, this may be an excellent time to check resistance readings in the fuel tank sender (see project 4, step 4).

Unbolt and remove the tank. This may be the most laborious part of the job, but the tank needs to come off.

Shake the tank to dislodge any contaminants.

3. Close the fuel tap or block off any tank outlets so the tank will hold liquid. Do not force anything in the opening that may damage or enlarge the opening. Put about 1 gallon of Varsol or other solvent in the tank, add a handful of pennies or clean bolts and nuts, and replace the fuel cap.

Shake the tank vigorously so the pennies or nuts and bolts have a chance to strike and dislodge any contamination in the tank.

Dump out the tank and repeat as necessary until the solvent comes out clean.

If the tank still does not look clean after this home remedy, it can be professionally cleaned with steam or chemicals. Ask at your tractor supply store for a cleaning location or look in your phone directory under "steam cleaning."

Reinstall the tank, but do not attach the fuel line yet. If you want to be absolutely certain the tank flows properly, connect a hose to the outlet with the other end of the hose plugged and ready above a suitable fuel container. Pour a gallon or two of fuel in the tank and observe whether it flows out as expected when the plug is removed.

Once the tank is clean, bolt it back on to the tractor and reattach all fuel lines and fuel gauge wires.

On this tractor the diesel fuel supply and return lines, plus level sender wires, are all located in one unit for quick assembly and service.

PROJECT 13	Replace Diesel Fuel Filter(s)

Time: 1 hour or less

Frequency: Every 100 hours or as needed

Tractor specs needed: May need fuel injection–system bleeding procedure

Special parts: New filters

Special tools: None

Materials: Pan to catch fuel, rags

Cost: Cost of filter(s)

Skill level: Easy

Tip: On the filter, mark the engine hours when it was changed or when it should be changed again.

Maintenance tip: Diesel fuel is lighter than water and floats above it when undisturbed, so water and sediment collect at the bottom of the tank overnight. Fill the fuel tank at the end of the day. Before starting the engine the next day, open the drain valve until only diesel fuel runs out. This removes water and the contaminants before they can plug up the fuel filter.

In a diesel engine, fuel filters play a crucial role in stopping dirt and other contaminants from damaging precisely machined surfaces and blocking the tiny passages in the fuel injection system. Fuel filters are cheap insurance against costly engine wear and breakdowns, so change them regularly.

Before you start, for diesel engines, you may need to bleed air out of the fuel lines after completing this project. This information is found in the manual, so have it handy or find out the correct procedure from a tractor mechanic or parts supplier.

Summer diesel can gel in cold weather and cause fuel filter blockage. If you are caught with a tank full of summer diesel in the winter, add the correct amount of anti-gel additive (left), available at fuel suppliers, to prevent blocked filters. At right the gasoline engine stabilizer is used to prevent gasoline from forming varnishlike sludge in filters and carburetors.

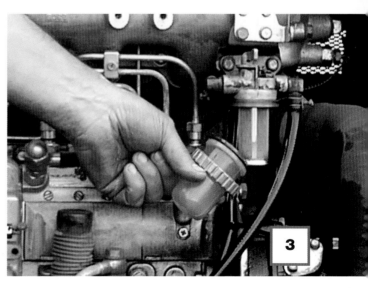

After the engine is completely cool, close the fuel tap.

1. Stop the engine. Letting it cool down completely is not absolutely essential, but it makes the work a lot more comfortable.

Close the fuel tap, which may be located at the bottom of the tank at the injector pump or at a separate pump in between, as on this Case-International 2096.

2. For tractors with a sediment bowl at the engine, unscrew the bowl. You can expect a lot of diesel to pour out at this point, so have a pan or absorbent material ready to catch the fuel.

3. Clean the bowl and any metal gauze pieces in fresh diesel fuel.

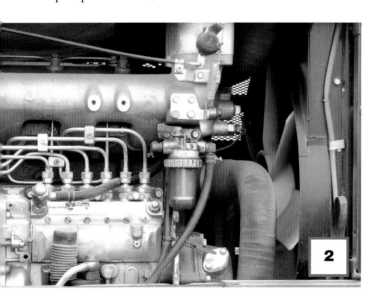

Unscrew the sediment bowl and remove.

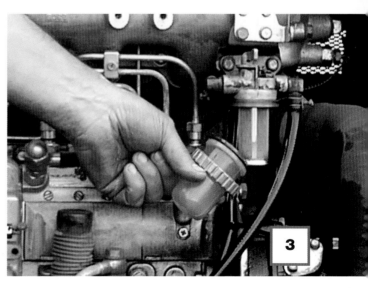

Clean the bowl in fresh diesel fuel.

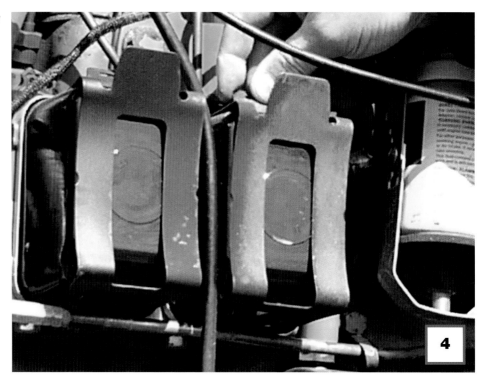

4. If the engine is equipped with cassette-type filters as shown, remove the filter by prying off the flat metal filter retaining spring and pulling the filter straight off.

5. Many diesel tractors use filters that consist of a replaceable element within a separate housing as shown.

To remove, unscrew the center bolt. Clean the housing thoroughly in diesel fuel. Replace any O-rings that come with the filter. If any rubber O-rings must be reused, inspect them for cracks or other damage and replace if there is any doubt to their condition.

6. At the bottom of cartridge-type fuel filters, there may be small drain screws. These can be periodically opened between filter changes to drain out water and other fuel contaminants, thus helping maintain high-efficiency filtering. And now that you know they are there, you can also use them to drain the filters before changing. Another type of fuel filter evacuator is shown on the spin-on-type fuel filters at right.

Place the new filter cartridge and O-rings in the filter housing and reattach to the engine. Replace the evacuator screws and sediment bowl and tighten everything securely.

Start the engine and check for fuel leaks. If moderate tightening does not cure a leak, stop the engine, remove the filter, and replace the gaskets or O-ring at the point of leakage.

Remove the filter by unscrewing the center bolt.

Small drain screws are at the bottom of cartridge-type fuel filters and can be periodically opened between filter changes to drain water and other contaminants.

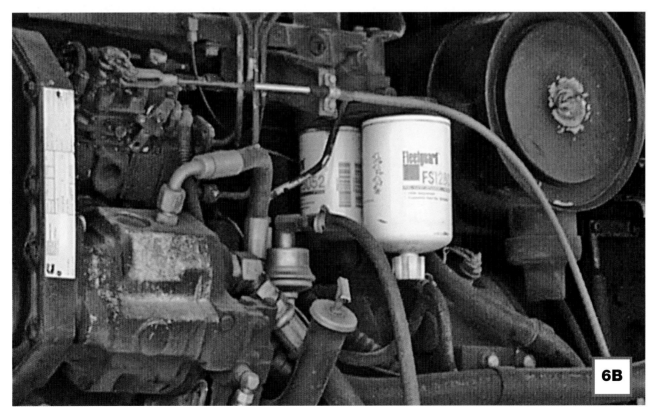

Drain screws on spin-on fuel filters.

| **PROJECT 14** | Replace Carburetor Float Valve |

Time: 3–4 hours

Frequency: As needed or every 3–4 seasons

Special parts: Carburetor overhaul kit

Information needed: Carburetor float height specification from service manual

Special tools: None

Materials: Carburetor cleaning spray, solvent, rags, brushes

Cost: About $25

Skill level: Difficult

Tip: To prevent damage to soft brass jets and other small passages inside the carburetor, use monofilament fishing line to poke out blockages.

Maintenance tip: Install or change the inline fuel filter as part of this procedure. If your gasoline-engine tractor does not presently have one, install one. They are cheap and easy to add on. Measure the outside diameter of the fuel line and buy a filter to fit that size of line. Cut out a section of fuel line about 1 inch longer than the filter and clamp the filter in place using the rubber hoses and clamps included with the fuel filter.

The carburetor on gasoline engines mixes fuel with air to provide efficient engine operation. In normal use the carburetor gives little trouble with only a few parts commonly wearing out, such as the needle valve, which is the subject of this project. Maintaining air and fuel filters is important because entry of dirt in the intake air or in the fuel can plug up passages and abrades precisely machined parts, such as the needle valve and seat.

Sitting idle for long periods is the worst enemy of efficient carburetor operation because gasoline inside the

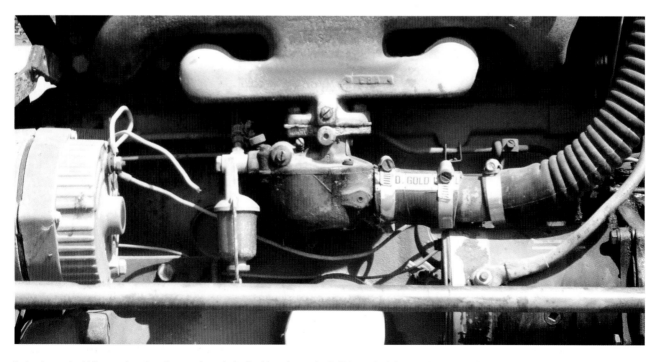

Carburetor overhaul kits come in various degrees of complexity. For this project, a simple kit is required: float needle and seat, float bowl gasket, and intake manifold gasket.

Detach the throttle and choke rods or cables.

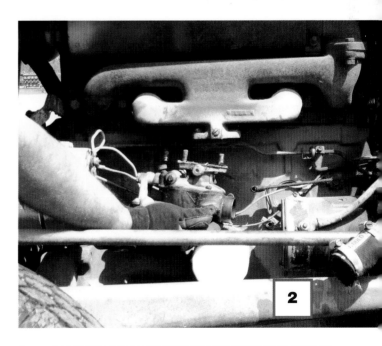

Unscrew the bolts that attach the carburetor to the engine and remove the carburetor.

To order the right kit, the tractor serial number is necessary but is not sufficient information. You'll also need the carburetor number, which is on a brass or aluminum tag somewhere on the carburetor body. It's hard to find and read once you find it, but you do need the number.

carburetor gradually turns into a varnishlike substance that clogs various passages.

Before you start, find out if the new needle and seat kit includes the specification for the float height. If not, determine the correct float height from the tractor service manual.

Don't adjust the mixture-adjusting screws at this point.

1. Most gasoline tractors use gravity to feed fuel to the carburetor and have a fuel shut-off valve at the tank. Close the fuel shut-off valve. If the engine has a fuel pump to move fuel, this step is probably not necessary. Loosen the nut or clamp that holds the fuel line and detach the fuel line. Loosen the clamp or remove the bolts that connect the intake air pipe and disconnect it.

Detach the throttle and choke rods or cables. If they are held on by what appears to be little ball-and-socket joints as shown, push forward slightly on the joint to open it and make room to pull out the ball end.

2. Undo the bolts that hold the carburetor to the engine and remove the carburetor. Stuff a rag in the

Remove the screws that connect the float bowl to the carburetor and remove the float bowl and its gasket.

engine intake to prevent dirt from falling into the carburetor. Outside (or in a well-ventilated area), use the carburetor spray or solvent to clean the interior and exterior of the carburetor.

Spray all bolts and screws thoroughly with penetrating oil. Small fasteners on the carburetor often seize in their threads. Penetrating oil helps get them out without breakage or rounding off the heads. Let the penetrating oil work for several minutes.

3. Do not disturb (yet) the two to three mixture-adjusting screws. These screws are often made of brass and have a small spring around their shaft to keep them in tension so they do not rotate on their own. Typical examples are the screws below and to the left of the word "Marvel" in the photo on page 72. If the screws are accidentally disturbed much beyond a half turn or so, you'll need to consult the tractor service manual on proper carburetor tuning procedure.

4. At the bottom of the carburetor is a large bowl-shaped piece—the "float bowl." Remove the screws or bolts that hold the float bowl to the carburetor and remove it and its gasket. You may need to wiggle the bowl a bit to get it off. Keep the old gasket as intact as possible so you can make sure the new one is correct.

Hold the carburetor upright, and by gently pushing up on the float, observe how it forces the small needle

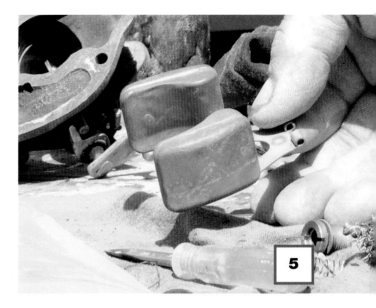

Remove the float hinge, float, and any other springs or brackets in the float area.

upward. This mimics what happens when gasoline flows into the bowl: the float rises and shuts off the flow (much like a toilet valve). As fuel is mixed with air for the engine to burn, the float lowers, the valve opens, and so on.

5. Turn the carburetor over so the float is facing up. Take a close look at the several small parts around the float pivot and compare them to the kit instruction sheet

Remove the needle valve.

so you know what goes back where. Make a sketch or notes if required.

Push out the small pin on the float hinge. Remove the float and extract any other springs and brackets in the pivot area.

Shake the float and listen if there is liquid sloshing around in it. If so, the float needs to be replaced or repaired. A float that does not float will not allow proper operation of the needle valve.

6. Pull out the needle valve that the float pushes. Using a large screwdriver or coin, unscrew the needle valve seat.

7. Close inspection of the needle will probably show a band of wear on the tapered end, which is formed as the needle repeatedly touches the seat. You may also be able to feel the ridges by dragging a fingernail lightly across the needle's end.

That worn area is what prevents a good seal when the float rises. Modern needle valves, like the one in this kit, often have a rubber tip for a better seal.

8. In this case the overhaul kit included a new low-speed mixture adjustment needle, shown beside the old one that is still in place. To determine the correct initial setting, count the number of turns (e.g., one and three

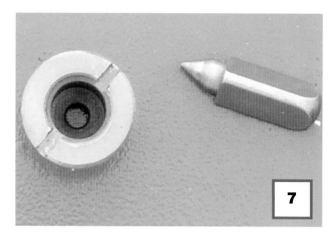

Check the needle valve for wear.

quarters) it takes to gently screw the old one in until it just touches bottom. You'll feel added resistance at that point. Record this measurement, then remove the old needle.

Gently screw in the new mixture screw until it just touches bottom. The end of this screw is finely pointed brass, so being too forceful can ruin it. Once you feel the added pressure when the screw bottoms, unscrew it the same number of turns as the old one took to reach bottom.

9. Screw in the new seat, including its gasket, and gently drop in the new needle.

Count the number of turns it takes to screw in an old adjustment needle until it touches the bottom.

Install the new seat and gasket and drop in the new needle.

10. Reattach the float and replace the springs and brackets mentioned in step 5. The new kit will probably also provide a new pivot pin to use.

Measure the float height as outlined in the carburetor kit instructions or the tractor manual. If it needs adjusting, use needle-nose pliers to bend the float arm to achieve the correct float height.

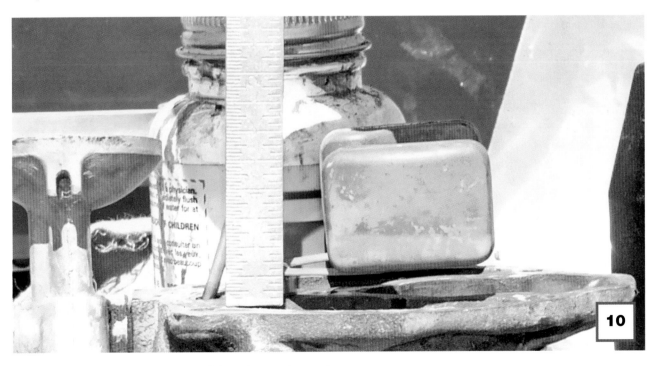

Measure the float height according to the carburetor kit instructions or tractor manual.

Replace the venturi tube, large gasket, and float bowl.

11. Place the venturi tube back in place. Lay the large gasket in place and wiggle the float bowl into place. You may find that the long, tapering mixture adjustment screw takes some finesse to slide into the tube. Replace the float bowl screws, tightening each a bit at a time so the gasket is compressed evenly.

12. Reattach the carburetor to the engine. Reattach the fuel line, intake pipe, throttle, and choke controls.

13. Open the valve on the bottom of the fuel tank and watch the carburetor for a few minutes. There should be no fuel oozing or dripping out from the

Reattach the carburetor to the engine.

Open the fuel tank valve and watch for any leaks.

carburetor body, which indicates a float valve sticking open. The sediment bowl and fuel line should also show no leaks. A gasoline leak could cause a fire during operation.

If the needle valve doesn't close properly, use the handle of a screwdriver to rap the carburetor a few times to shake the valve free. If the problem persists, open up the carburetor again, starting from step 1, and correct the problem. Usually the trouble involves dirt or bits of gasket material stuck in the needle valve.

MAKING GASKETS

If gaskets are not readily available (or the one that came in the kit gets broken), it is possible to make a replacement. Sheets of gasket material in various thicknesses and materials are sold at tractor and auto supply stores, either as a variety pack or in rolls of material made of specific thickness and material.

Many types of "gasket in a tube" are now available, and the sealing performance can actually be an improvement on older tractors. If you use this type of gasket, be sure to get the right kind for the type of fluid that needs to be sealed. Ask your parts supplier about the type they recommend because formulations are constantly improving. When you use this type of gasket maker, follow the directions exactly. For example, you may need to give the pieces a few minutes to set up before tightening the bolts. Skip a step and you may end up with a frustrating leak.

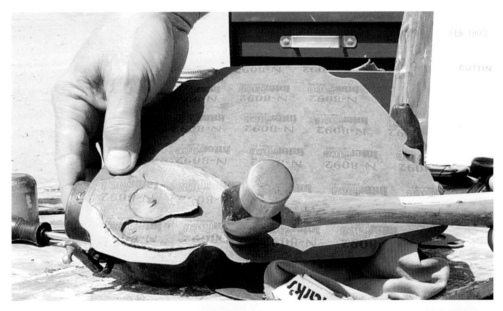

Place the sheet over the part to be sealed and gently tap on the sheet to transfer the pattern to the sheet.

Where possible, punch out the bolt/screw holes first so that during subsequent cutting, the gasket is pinned in position by using the bolts/screws. Use hollow punches (available at hardware stores) to cut round holes.

With the gasket pinned in place by the bolts, use a sharp hobby knife to cut the necessary areas.

With a little patience, intricate shapes can be formed. Leave extra material around the outside because it can be trimmed away once the parts are assembled.

Make sure no important holes are covered. Use the old gasket, even if it's torn, as reference for what's covered and what's not.

With gasket material on hand, a little tracing and cutting can keep you going if you run across a leaky part in the middle of a job.

It's not factory perfect, but it does the job and eliminates waiting for back-ordered or unavailable parts.

PROJECT 15 | Replace Muffler

Time: 1 hour

Frequency: As needed

Tractor specs needed: None

Special parts: New muffler and clamps

Special tools: None

Materials: Exhaust system cement

Cost: About $25 to $50

Skill level: Easy

Tip: Exhaust system fasteners are always rusted and seized, so use plenty of penetrating oil and give it time to work in before trying to remove them.

Maintenance tip: Every now and then tap the muffler lightly with a wrench or other metal tool. If the sound is a dull thud rather than a sharp metallic clang, the muffler is probably rusting out and a replacement should be scheduled.

Tractor mufflers eventually rust and fall apart due to moisture condensation, corrosive components in the exhaust gasses, and engine-generated vibration. For the sake of preserving your own hearing, an inoperative muffler should be replaced. Mufflers also incorporate devices to arrest sparks in the exhaust that could fly out and ignite dry crops or grasses. Tractor mufflers, even for older tractors, are available from tractor parts suppliers.

Inlet and outlet markings on a replacement muffler. The inlet end pipe is also generally slotted to allow the clamp to squeeze it firmly against the engine outlet pipe.

This replacement muffler is a straight-through design that permits free-exhaust gas flow, but does not arrest sparks. If your tractor is operated around dry, combustible materials, use a spark-arresting muffler.

If your tractor has a spark-arrester muffler equipped with clean-out plugs as shown, periodically remove the plugs while the muffler is cold and run the engine at fast idle to blow out trapped carbon. If a crust of carbon has formed over the holes, poke it loose. Replace plugs after you clean out the muffler and use anti-seize to prevent further corrosion.

81

Remove the old muffler and clean any scale off the exhaust manifold stub.

1. Remove muffler clamp. Due to heat-induced corrosion, the bolts will probably break off. This is why you will also be installing new clamps.

Pull off the old muffler. This may take some wiggling and twisting due to corrosion. Standing on the hood helps give you good leverage on the muffler at the top. Heating with a plumber's propane torch is okay, after all, this area gets plenty of heat when in use.

For this tractor, it was already without a muffler and had a stub exhaust.

2. Test fit the muffler on to the exhaust outlet. You may need to scrape the corrosion in order to fit the new muffler. If the fit is a bit inexact, some muffler cement can be used to seal loose areas.

3. Slip the new clamp over the muffler inlet, then slide the new muffler on to the exhaust opening. Apply anti-seize compound to the clamp threads and tighten securely.

Above right: *Use muffler cement to seal loose areas.*

Right: *Slide the new muffler onto the new clamp on the exhaust opening.*

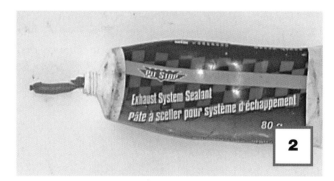

PROJECT 16	Install Exhaust Weather Cap

Time: 15 minutes

Frequency: One time

Tractor specs needed: None

Special parts: Exhaust cap

Special tools: None

Special materials: None

Cost: About $5

Skill level: Very easy

Tip: Before you buy a tractor exhaust cap, measure the actual outlet pipe diameter on the muffler so you can buy a cap to fit that diameter.

Maintenance tip: When you put the tractor in storage at the end of the season, spray some lubricant on the exhaust cap pivot.

When a tractor sits idle outside, exhaust pipes that point upward can collect rainwater. Birds and wasps have been known to nest in tractor exhausts that have been left for several days. A simple exhaust cap can prevent unwanted contamination and intruders.

When the engine is stopped, gravity holds the cap shut. When the engine is started, the pressure of the exhaust gasses forces the cap open so it does not interfere with exhaust gas flow and engine power.

Caps aplenty. Tractors of the era covered in this book were typically fitted with a vertical outlet and a weather cap as described in this project. Probably to save assembly costs, tractors now usually come with a simple curved outlet. It keeps most of the rain out, but not the critters.

If the caps are worn out, corroded, or banged up during work, they need lubrication or replacement so they can perform their proper function.

1

Check for corrosion on the muffler outlet.

84

1. Check the end of the muffler outlet to make sure the metal is not thin from excessive corrosion. Pressing on it with your fingers should not be able to bend the metal. If necessary, cut the outlet a bit shorter to expose solid metal.

2. Place the exhaust cap on the muffler outlet with the tab of the cap facing the operator's seat.

3. Tighten the clamp securely.

Put the exhaust cap on the muffler outlet.

Tighten and secure the clamp.

CHAPTER 5
LUBRICATION SYSTEM

The tractor's lubrication system involves engine oil, transmission-differential-hydraulic (TDH) oil, and grease for isolated joints.

For engines, you have a choice of synthetic or mineral (petroleum-based) oils. Actually both are made from petroleum, but the difference (aside from various manufacturers' additive packages) is in how much they are processed and the consistency of the resultant molecular size distribution. Discuss with your lubricant supplier what a synthetic oil can accomplish in your tractor and whether the cost difference makes economic sense for the age of your tractor and its use. Semi-synthetic blended oils are also available at a lower cost than 100 percent synthetics.

At this writing there are no biodegradable oils for use in engines, but major manufacturers do have biodegradable greases and hydraulic oils. These oils are made from vegetable oil bases and developed for marine and forestry applications where water and soil pollution must be avoided.

CHANGE TDH OIL TOO

The much larger amount of oil involved (about 7 gallons even in a small tractor) and its cost often leads to owners putting off this part of necessary maintenance. That's very unwise because the transmission, differentials, and hydraulic system are probably the most time-consuming and costly to repair, and it's not the sort of project that can be done by most owners.

For dependable tractor life and lower overall operating cost, change the TDH fluid and filter according to its schedule. Aside from making the change after the first 50 (or other recommended) hours of use of a new tractor, this task isn't required very often—only every 750 hours or annually. If you've bought a used tractor and aren't certain the TDH oil was maintained properly, change it now and keep to a recommended lubrication schedule thereafter. It may seem expensive, but it's minor compared to a transmission or hydraulic pump rebuild.

Above and opposite: Wherever possible, review the greasing recommendations in the tractor manual because there may be more involved than pumping in grease. Some bearings, such as the front axle pivot on this Kubota tractor, require removal of a breather port plug. Apply grease until it oozes from the breather port, and then replace the plug.

PROJECT 17 | Greasing

Time: 15 minutes

Frequency: Daily, weekly, or monthly

Tractor specs needed: Any detailed greasing procedures

Special parts: None

Special tools: Grease gun

Materials: Wiping rag

Cost: None

Skill level: Very easy

Tip: Mark the recommended greasing interval (10, 50, or 100 hours) at the fitting.

Maintenance tip: The type of grease is important, so ask your lubricant supplier or tractor parts store staff for what they recommend. In general, a good-quality extreme pressure (EP) grease is good for tractor and implement lubrication.

Many of the tractor's moving parts (e.g., steering arms) are isolated from any lubrication reservoir so they depend on greasing to maintain movement and minimize wear. Tractors have several fittings ("zerks," after their Austrian-American inventor, Oscar Zerk), which require application of grease at intervals of 10, 50, or 100 hours. In regular use, those correspond to daily, weekly, or monthly greasing.

Too much grease can be as bad or worse for a bearing as undergreasing, so pay attention to the correct schedule and amount of grease. One to four pump-strokes is usually enough. Pumping the grease gun until fresh grease runs out can stretch the bearing seals and create an entry point for dirt and lead to early failure. Regular application of small amounts of grease is much better for the bearing.

1. Clean off the fitting so dirt is not forced into the bearing.

Clean the dirt off the fitting.

Push the grease gun
end onto the fitting.

2. Push the grease gun end on to the fitting. You should be able to hear and feel a slight snap when it is fully in place.

3. Pump the grease gun once or twice to apply grease. If a ribbon of clean grease curls out beside the fitting, the grease gun is not aligned with the zerk. When the grease gun end is lined up straight with the fitting, all the grease will pump into the bearing.

Pump in two to four shots of grease, and stop if old grease starts to ooze out of the bearing. Continue for all grease points.

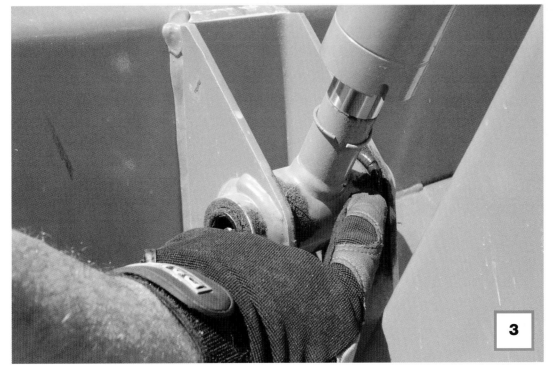

Pump the grease gun
one or two times to
apply grease.

PROJECT 18 | Change Oil and Filter

Time: 1 hour or less

Frequency: Every 100 engine hours

Tractor specs needed: Tractor manual oil type, quantity, and viscosity

Special parts: Oil, filters

Special tools: Oil filter wrench (for spin-on filters only)

Materials: Rubber gloves, large drain pan, rags

Cost: About $40 for engine oil and filters

Skill level: Easy

Tip: In heavy-duty engines, oil is best drained when hot so the contaminants remain in suspension. Since that means handling an equally hot oil drain plug and a risk of getting splashed with hot oil, wear heavy gloves and apparel with sleeves to prevent burns. Silicone oven mitts are good heatproof protection.

Maintenance tip: If the tractor is in continuous use, oil filters may not need changing with every oil change—check your manual for recommendations. If the tractor is used less than 100 to 150 hours per season, changing the oil filter along with the oil is an inexpensive insurance policy against wear.

Your tractor needs regular engine oil changes because over time the antiwear additives in engine oil break down and corrosive liquids accumulate in the engine oil. The accumulation of contaminants is worse in engines that are run under light loads or idled for long periods.

Be sure to obtain the right type of oil for your machine. For large, heavy-duty diesel engines, a straight-grade oil such as 30W is often specified, while others require a multiweight oil. Check in your manual and with your lubricant supplier for recommendations.

There are different drain plugs and filter locations for changing the TDH lubricant, but the procedure is similar to changing the engine oil: drain, change filters, and refill. Some tractors may have more than one TDH drain plug, so check the manual. Since the quantity of oil is much larger (check manual for capacity), make sure you have a big enough pan to catch the oil.

Before you start, make sure the tractor is fully warmed up—at the end of an hour or more of work is best.

1. Position the drain pan under the oil drain plug and loosen but don't remove the plug. When the drain plug can be turned by hand, put on a glove and turn the plug the rest of the way to remove. The plug will almost always shoot out of your hand and into the dirty oil, but don't worry, you can fish it out once the oil cools. Let the oil drain at least 15 minutes.

2. Position the oil pan under the oil filter(s). Place rags under the filters because some oil is sure to drip down. Remove the filters by loosening the center retaining bolt.

Remove the oil plug and drain for at least 15 minutes.

Remove oil filter by unscrewing the center fastening bolt.

3. For spin-on-type oil filters, turn the case. You'll need a suitable-sized filter wrench to turn these large-diameter filters.

4. Replace any O-rings supplied with the new cartridge-type filter. Apply a coating of fresh oil to the rubber gaskets on the base of the filters (either type), then install the new filters. Wipe up any spilled oil so new leaks, if any, will be clearly visible.

5. Reinstall the drain plug. Make absolutely sure it turns easily by hand. Many oil change projects go bad at this point because the plug is carelessly cross-threaded and tightened from the start with a wrench, which destroys the threads in the oil pan. This results in a bothersome and expensive repair job.

Once the plug threads in easily about halfway, use a wrench to tighten the plug. Use the specified torque, if known. Otherwise tighten until it contacts metal, then about 1/8th turn more. Refill with the specified amount and type of new engine oil.

If you have a spin-on oil filter, you will need a filter wrench to remove the filter.

Apply fresh oil to the rubber gaskets on the base of the filters.

6. Mark the engine hour reading and/or date on the filter, so that during the routine daily service you can see when it will need its next change. Start and run the tractor. The oil pressure light or gauge should indicate normal operation shortly after starting.

Examine the drain plug area and filter bases to make sure there is no leakage. If there is a small leak, see if a slight tightening of the plug, retaining bolt, or filter cures it. If not, stop the engine and correct the leakage. Typical causes include a bad drain-plug gasket, cross-threaded drain plug, or twisted/torn filter gaskets.

Write the date and time of the filter change directly on the filter so you know when its next service is due.

PROJECT 19 | Fix a Hydraulic Hose Leak

Time: About 15 minutes for a simple leak

Frequency: As needed

Tractor specs needed: None

Special parts: None

Special tools: None required

Materials: Pipe thread sealing tape

Cost: About $2 for tape, $8 to $20 for a new hose

Skill level: Easy

Tip: Do not use only cable ties (zip ties) or wire to secure or bundle hydraulic hoses. They do not allow hoses to expand and contract with pressure and eventually chafe through the hose. Instead, use hydraulic hose straps and/or apply a textile sleeve around the hoses.

Maintenance tip: To pinpoint oil leaks, spray antiperspirant on the oily area. Fresh leaks will show up clearly on the white surface.

The tractor's hydraulic system provides the power to make heavy lifting as easy as moving a small control lever. However, the fluid under high pressure that makes hydraulic movement possible also occasionally tends to escape out of tiny holes and loose connectors, which makes a mess and reduces the overall efficiency of the system.

Some of the leaks are due to faulty gaskets or seals and can be repaired with the procedures in project 20. Many of the leaks are due to leaking hoses and hose connectors and are easily put right with attention to sealing the leakage paths.

Oil leaks, especially from hydraulic hoses, are both a performance and environmental problem. Thread sealing tape is a soft gasketlike material used to prevent fluid leakage from threaded joints, such as this hydraulic line. For tractor thread sealing jobs, the newer pink material performs better than the older white or blue tapes.

If the leak is from the hose itself, remove the hose as described in step 1 and obtain a replacement. Reattach as described in steps 2 and 3.

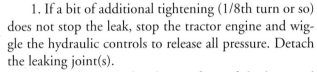

Tighten the fittings lightly to see if the leaks stop.

Wrap thread sealing tape tightly around the threads.

1. If a bit of additional tightening (1/8th turn or so) does not stop the leak, stop the tractor engine and wiggle the hydraulic controls to release all pressure. Detach the leaking joint(s).

Inspect the tapered sealing surfaces of the hose and where it attaches to the fitting. The leak may be due to contamination, which can be wiped off. If there are deep scratches or pits, you may have to replace the damaged part.

If you are leaving the system open for more than a few minutes, stuff shop rags in the open holes to prevent the entry of dirt.

2. Wrap one or two layers of thread sealing tape tightly around the threads. Start from the top and wind clockwise to the bottom, stretching the tape as you wind so it forms itself into the threads. Remove any tape that covers the openings.

3. Remove any plugs you had placed in the joints and tighten the new hose securely. For rigid metal hydraulic lines, make sure both ends can be successfully attached before you fully tighten either end.

Remove any plugs in the joints and tighten the new hose.

PROJECT 20	Replace a Leaking Gasket

Time: Depends on the difficulty of unbolting the gasketed parts

Frequency: As needed

Tractor specs needed: None

Special parts: New gasket

Special tools: Gasket scraper, torque wrench

Materials: None

Cost: Cost of gasket

Skill level: Medium difficulty

Tip: If the gasket is no longer manufactured or waiting for a back-ordered part will hold up critical work, you can often make a gasket from suitable material—refer to project 14 for a description of how to do it.

Maintenance tip: Blown gaskets are often the result of excess pressure as a result of overfilling a system with oil or coolant.

Gaskets are pieces of soft material sandwiched between stationary metal surfaces. The soft faces of the gaskets conform to very small hills and hollows in the metal surfaces to seal in oil and seal out dirt.

Gasket material depends on the sealing job to be done and the conditions under which the bolted joint is expected to operate, so replace the failed gasket with a new gasket of the right material. Exhaust system gaskets,

Clean the area before you start the project.

Remove the part where the leak occurs.

for example, need to be able to operate between very hot parts. Even what appears to be a simple rubber O-ring may be a specially chosen nitrile, Viton, or other special-performance polymer. You will need to buy the right part to get the right performance.

Seals are pieces of soft material that prevent fluid leakage between a rotating/sliding surface and a stationary surface, such as between a rotating wheel and a stationary axle. The lips of the seal conform to very small hills and hollows in the metal surfaces to seal in oil and seal out dirt. The seal profile may range from the torus (doughnut) shape of an O-ring to complex multi-lip seals. Seals may be all soft material or stiffened with metal. Oils and coolants contain additives that soften and preserve seals. These additives are one of the things that break down over time, which is another reason for regular oil changes.

Before you start, inspect the area to determine if the gasket is above or below the normal fluid level in the case being sealed. If the gasket is below normal, drain out enough fluid so it does not gush out when you unbolt the parts.

1. Clean the area before starting so dirt does not fall inside when you unbolt the gasketed parts. There is more than one leak here. Several leaks turned out to be leaking fuel pipes, which have no gaskets. These leaks were repaired as described in project 19.

2. Clean the area and unbolt the parts where the leak occurs. If it seems to be taking much greater than expected force to turn the bolts, do not apply more force—this could snap the bolts off and make the job much harder. Before you apply big muscle:

Spray on plenty of penetrating oil and give it some time to work into the threads.

Rap the top of the bolt head with a punch or the ball end of a ball-peen hammer. The blow can help free the bolt from corrosion in the threads.

When you get the bolts out, inspect the threads. If you see corrosion or galling (metal that appears to be torn off), screw a tap or oiled bolt down the threaded hole to clean the threads. If you are in doubt about the bolt condition, replace it with one of the correct length and grade.

Remove the gasket with a gasket scraper to avoid damaging the metal surfaces.

Pin the gasket in place with the attachment bolts.

Turn the tractor on and examine the area for leaks.

3. Use a gasket scraper to completely remove the old gasket without scratching the metal surfaces.

4. Put the gasket in place on the part with the bolts so it is held in place. If using gasket sealer, apply it to one side of the gasket and stick it in place. Apply sealer to the other side of the gasket and align the metal parts of the joint. Press and wiggle the joint slightly to squeeze the gasket sealer evenly over the gasket and into the metal surfaces.

Apply a dab of anti-seize compound on the bolt threads, or if the joint is subject to loosening from vibration, use thread-locking compound instead.

Tighten bolts by hand and then tighten each bolt a bit at a time. Use specified torque if known, or refer to the general torque values charts in chapter 1.

If you used gasket sealer, wait a few minutes for it to cure. Replace any fluids that were drained.

5. Start and run the tractor to inspect for leakage. In this case, holes drilled through the bolt heads indicate the bolts should have been secured with safety wire and a seal to indicate the injection pump had only been serviced by an authorized fuel-injection pump shop. It is something to inspect when you consider buying a used diesel tractor.

PROJECT 21 | Repack and Adjust Wheel Bearings (Two-Wheel Drive)

Time: 1–2 hours

Frequency: Every two to three years

Tractor specs needed: Castle nut torque

Special parts: New grease seals

Special tools: Wheel-bearing greaser, torque wrench

Materials: Grease

Cost: About $10 for seals alone, about $25 per set of two new bearings, if needed

Skill level: Moderately difficult

Tip: If your tractor is equipped with a front-end loader, tilt the bucket straight down and lower the loader fully to jack the front wheels off the ground, then secure with blocks.

Maintenance tip: Periodically check wheel bearing conditions and bearing adjustment by lifting the front wheels off the ground, giving the wheels a spin, and trying to shake the wheel while grasping it at the top and bottom. If there is a noticeable roughness or looseness, it's time to pay attention to the wheel bearings.

Two-wheel-drive field and utility tractors need periodic lubrication of the front wheel bearings. Some models are equipped with zerk fittings, but even those occasionally need to have the bearings removed, cleaned, and repacked with fresh grease and adjusted for proper free play.

The lubrication process also involves setting and adjusting the bearing by tightening the retaining nut. For anyone who has adjusted the wheel, steering hub, or hub bearings in a bicycle, this process will be quite familiar.

Wheel bearings on highway vehicles are lubricated with a special wheel-bearing grease. However, since tractors do not travel at high road speeds, a good-quality, extreme pressure (EP) grease, which is used for the other grease fittings on tractors and implements, can give satisfactory service.

1

Loosen the front wheel bolts.

Lift the front wheels with a jack and use jack stands or wood blocks to support the tractor.

Remove the wheel's dust cap.

Use a dust-cap removal tool to pry off pressed-in caps.

1. Loosen the front wheel bolts slightly, just enough that they can be turned easily with the wrench.

2. Lift the front wheels off the ground and support the tractor with jack stands or solid wood blocks. DO NOT rely on the jack alone to keep the tractor supported. If it falls, there will be severe damage to you and the tractor. Fully remove the wheel bolts and wheels.

3. Remove the dust cap in the center of the wheel to expose the wheel-bearing retaining nut. On this tractor, bolts hold the cap on. Other models may have a pressed-in cap that can removed by carefully prying it off or using a dust-cap removal tool (about $15 at auto supply stores).

4. The hub-retaining nut is prevented from turning by a wire cotter pin. Straighten the pin and remove it.

Straighten the wire cotter pin and remove it.

Remove the hub to expose the spindle.

5. Remove the retaining nut, thrust washer, and outer bearing. Place them in solvent to soak.

6. Pull the hub straight off the axle shaft to expose the spindle. Be ready to support the weight. The hub may weigh up to about 50 pounds on large tractors. The outer wheel bearing may fall free during the process. Don't worry, it has to be removed anyway.

7. To remove the inner (large) wheel bearing from the hub, pry out the grease retaining seal and discard. Put bearing in solvent to soak.

Remove the inner wheel bearing and pry out the grease retaining seal.

Clean the spindle.

8. Clean the bearing axle (spindle).

9. Inspect the clean bearings for missing rollers or heavy wear, as indicated by shiny spots or flat spots on the rollers. This bearing shows score marks where a particle of contamination has worn.

Also inspect the race (surface on which the rollers bear) inside the hub. If there is damage or very heavy wear, it may be worthwhile to buy a set of new bearings and races.

If you are going to buy new bearings and races, take the clean hubs with you to the tractor supply store to

Check the bearings and race for damage.

have the races pressed out and the new ones pressed in. This can be done in the home shop with a hammer, heavy punches, and a hardwood block, but it's vastly simpler, cleaner, faster, and safer to have it done by a shop with heavy-duty tools and equipment.

If you are reusing the bearings, clean and dry them thoroughly. If you dry the bearings with compressed air, do not make them spin so rapidly that they make a siren sound—this severely damages roller bearings.

10. Place the clean wheel bearing between the plates of the lubricator and pump in grease until all the spaces in the bearing are filled. To speed things up, fill the central cavity of the bearing with grease. This must be filled before the lubricator will start forcing grease into the bearing. Do the smaller (outer) bearings first and then move on to the larger bearings with larger center cavities.

Dabbing some grease on your palm and working it into the bearing can also repack wheel bearings. Make sure grease is packed between every roller.

11. With the large hole of the hub upward, place the grease-packed inner (large) wheel bearing in position. Lightly grease the rim of the new grease seal and place it squarely on the hub. Using a wooden block to prevent damage to the seal, drive the new seal into position.

Pack the bearings with new grease.

Tip the hub up so the spindle hole is horizontal and place the small outer bearing in position. Fill the space between the bearings with grease and lightly grease the spindle.

Using your thumbs to keep the outer bearing in place, carefully place the hub squarely back on the axle

Drive the new seal into position by using a wooden block to prevent damage.

12

After the hub is back on the axle, replace the thrust washer and castle nut.

shaft. Twist the hub as you push it on so that the lips of the seal seat properly.

12. When the hub is fully on, replace the thrust washer and castle nut. The slots in the top of the castle nut allow insertion of the cotter pin to keep the retaining nut in position. Tighten the nut just enough to hold the hub in position—final adjustments will be made once the wheel is on.

13. Replace the wheel and tighten the lug bolts snugly, just enough that the wheel does not shift around on the hub as you turn the wheel. The complete tightening will be done once the wheel is back on the ground.

While slowly turning the wheel, tighten the castle nut to about 35 foot-pounds of torque or the value specified in the service manual. Then loosen the nut by one to one-half slots.

There are holes in the axle shaft every 90 degrees, so one of the slots should be very close to lining up with a hole. Align with the closest hole and replace the cotter pin and bend the ends over to hold it in place.

Reattach the dust cover, lower the wheels to the ground, and do the final tightening of the lug bolts.

13

Place the wheel back on the axle shaft and tighten the lugs.

CHAPTER 6
FUNCTIONALITY

To maintain its usefulness, the tractor has to be able to develop its rated pulling/pushing power, get to and from the field, and allow the operator to efficiently perform desired tasks. The projects in this section help maintain this overall functionality of the machine.

Suitcase weights are a popular way to add weight to the front end, but take into account the distance of the weights from the front axle. Adding a lot of weight ahead of the front axle adds an upward force to the rear due to the lever effect.

Bolt-on wheel weights put weight directly at the driving axle, such as on this loader-equipped tractor. Inexpensive calcium-chloride solution can be pumped into tires for added weight, but check your manual and with a local tire shop on whether this is advisable for your tractor.

PROJECT 22	Ballasting for Best Traction

Time: 15 minutes

Frequency: As needed

Tractor specs needed: Present weight, maximum operating weight

Special parts: Ballast weights, if needed

Special tools: Measuring tape

Materials: Stakes to mark beginning and end of run

Cost: Moderate

Skill level: Easy

Tip: A helper is required to drive the tractor.

Maintenance tip: As you become familiar with slippage measurement and results, you may be able to get a close estimate of slippage by inspecting the tire tracks. An overballasted tractor (too little slippage) leaves clear, distinct tread marks in the soil, while an underballasted tractor (too much slippage) smears the tread marks beyond recognition.

It might seem like the big, deep-lugged tires and heavy weight of your tractor are designed to achieve 100 percent hookup to the ground. But tractors are actually designed to work with tire slippage of 8 to 16 percent, depending on soil condition and whether the tractor is two-wheel drive, front-wheel assist, or four-wheel drive.

Achieving proper slippage is controlled mainly by ballasting (adding or subtracting weight), as well as by minor variations in speed. Adding ballast decreases slippage, while reducing ballast increase slippage. Given the same load, a minor increase in speed reduces slippage, while slowing down slightly increases it.

Too much slippage:

- The tractor can't seem to pull as much load as others of the same model.
- Tread bars (lugs) on the tractor tires seem to wear out quickly.

Not enough slippage:

- When starting off while pulling an implement, the tractor's front tires jerk upward, steering feels very light, and the tractor seems to "power hop" (i.e., driving tires repeatedly grab and spin).
- In the field, the tractor seems sluggish and burns more fuel than expected.
- Drive-tire lugs remain square and hardly worn, but final drives (gear case closest to drive wheels) get very hot while in use or wear out sooner than expected.

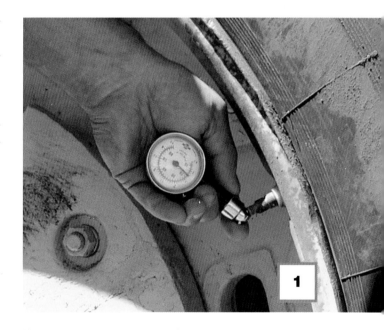

Use a pressure gauge to check the tire inflation pressure.

1. Set tire inflation pressure to factory-recommended pressure from the manual, a dealer, or a tire shop. Correct tire inflation is key to eliminating power hop and highway lope (rocking or bobbing motion). There may be ballast fluid in the tires, so make sure the inflation valve is above the level of the liquid.

Do not rely on the pressure recommendations molded into the side of the tire. Those pressures are maximum pressures not to be exceeded and used only at maximum load. Using these pressures at less than maximum load can reduce both tractor pulling power and tire life.

When checking tractor tire inflation, use a pressure gauge that's meant for measuring the low pressures used in tractor tires—typically under 20 psi. A gauge error of 2 psi wouldn't have much performance impact on a 30-psi car tire or 60-psi truck tire. But with a 14-psi tractor tire, a 2-psi gauge error represents too much uncertainty in actual pressure.

2. Consult the manual to find out the manufacturer's recommendations for the maximum weight of your tractor and the amount of weight that can be added. Overloading will make the tractor feel sluggish, increase the risk of the tire slipping on the rim, and increase risk of drivetrain damage.

DIMENSIONS:		
Wheel Base	88-3/4 Inches	94-11/16 Inches
Length Overall (Approx.)	146 Inches	152 Inches
Width Overall (Approx.)	79"	
Overall Height (Top of Cab)	—	76-1/2 Inches
Wheel Tread — Front	56" to 88"	
Wheel Tread — Rear	60" to 96"	
Turning Radius (W/O brakes)	Approximately 12 Ft.	Approximately 13'2
Ground Clearance (Min. under		
drawbar — approx.)	16 Inches	
Shipping Weight (Approx.)	7,000 lbs.	8,450 lbs.
Max. Operating Weight	11,000 lbs.	12,000 lbs.
TIRES:		
Front	7.50-16, F2, Tubeless — 6 Ply Rating	
	10.00-16, F2, Tubeless — 6 Ply Rating	
	9.5L-15, F2, Tubeless — 6 Ply Rating	
Rear	15.5-38, R1, Tubeless — 8 Ply Rating	
	16.9-34, R1 — 6 Ply Rating	
	16.9-38, R1, Tubeless — 6 Ply Rating	
	18.4-26, R1, Tubeless — 6 Ply Rating	

2

Check the owner's manual for the maximum weight of your tractor.

3

Make a mark at the bottom of a rear-drive tire.

109

Place a stake at the mark and have an assistant drive far enough ahead so that the tire revolves 20 times.

3. Using chalk or another suitable method, make a prominent mark at the bottom of a rear-drive tire.

Example: under load, tractor drive wheel turns 23.5 times. Slip equals 15 percent for 23 turns, plus 0.5 x (20-15) = 2.5, so total slip is 17.5 percent.

4. Place a stake at the mark. Have your assistant drive the tractor forward with the implement out of the ground. Mark the distance it takes for the tractor to move forward 20 full revolutions of the marked tire. Then have the operator drive forward the same distance with the implement in the ground. Count the number of turns the tires make and determine the slippage from

this table (For parts of a turn, take an equal part of the difference between full-turn percentages):

5a. Two-wheel-drive tractor weight balance: about 30 percent front/70 percent rear.

5b. True four-wheel- drive tractor (equal-size front and rear wheels) weight balance is about 55 percent front/45 percent rear.

5c. Weight balance for this type of tractor is usually 40 percent front/60 percent rear, and slippage rates are different for front and rear axles.

When adding or removing weight, the goal is to keep weight correctly balanced front to rear for each type of tractor. For example, if you add 200 pounds to a two-wheel-drive tractor, add 60 pounds to the front and 140 pounds to the rear to maintain the correct balance.

For this project, it's assumed that the tractor was in balance to begin with. If you want to be certain, get exact front, rear, and total weights by putting the tractor on the scale at a local elevator, livestock yard, or gravel-pit weigh station.

An additional slippage observation is needed for four-wheel-drive tractors that have front wheels smaller than the rear wheels (mechanical front-wheel drive, MFWD) or front-wheel assist (FWA). Major tire manufacturers advise that different slippage rates are needed for front and rear axles.

Revolutions under load	Percent slippage
20	0
21	5
22	10
23	15
24	20
25	25

The weight balance for a two-wheel-drive tractor is about 30 percent front and 70 percent rear.

FUNCTIONALITY

This positive front-tire slippage, overrun, or over-speed ranges from +1 to +5 percent. It helps maximize front-tire pulling efficiency, maintain good steering ability, and reduce tire wear. Consult the manual for the recommended range for your tractor and repeat steps 3 and 4 for the front axle to set proper positive front-tire slippage.

The weight balance for a four-wheel-drive tractor is about 55 percent front and 45 percent rear.

5B

5C

This tractor has a weight balance of about 40 percent front and 60 percent rear.

PROJECT 23	Brake Adjustment

Time: 1/2 hour or less

Frequency: Every 100 hours/yearly

Tractor specs needed: Brake free play and where to measure it

Special parts: None

Special tools: None

Materials: None

Required information: Brake free play specification from manual

Cost: None

Skill level: Easy

Tip: While adjusting the brake rods underneath the tractor, lubricate the brake pedal pivots so that they operate freely.

Tractor brakes need periodic inspection and adjustment of free play, which is the distance you can push the brake pedal with finger pressure before you feel it engaging the brake. Too much free play means the brakes won't be strong enough. Too little free play means the brakes will drag during use and wear out the brakes too quickly.

Tractor brakes are fairly easy to adjust because those from the era covered by this book usually use mechanical activation. If you've ever adjusted hand brakes on a bicycle, the process will be familiar—it's just on a much larger scale. On tractors, a rod from each pedal pulls on the brake for that side. Getting the pedals to exert equal force is a matter of adjusting the length of each rod.

Tractors have individual brake pedals for left and right brakes. The reason for this is so that at slow speeds in the field or under heavy pulling, individual brake pedals can be pressed to help slew the tractor around in a tight turn, such as at the end of a row while planting corn.

At higher speeds on the road or around the yard, the brake pedals are locked together so equal braking force is available from both sides. But if one side is out of adjustment and delivers less braking force than the other, the tractor may unexpectedly slew to one side when the brakes are applied together. This can be dangerous if, for example, the tractor is headed downhill on a slippery slope with a good-sized load in the bucket of the front-end loader.

1. Park the tractor on flat ground, remove the keys, and block the front wheels so it does not roll accidentally. Unlock the brakes from each other by lifting the locking lever.

2. Measure from some convenient fixed point to the face of the brake pedals in their normal resting position and record the measurement.

3. Press on each brake pedal by hand until you feel some resistance as the brake engages. This distance is the free play. Measuring from the same point as in step 1, record the distance to the face of the brake pedal. Repeat for the other brake pedal.

For each pedal, free play should be no more than 1/8 inch (3 mm) different. That way braking force will be equal when the brakes are applied together.

In this case, free play was equal but one brake pedal was not returning all the way when brakes were

After the wheels are secured and stable, unlock the brakes by lifting the locking lever.

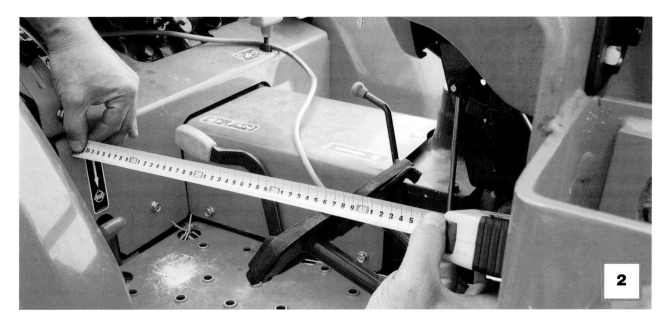

Measure the brake pedal distances in their normal resting position.

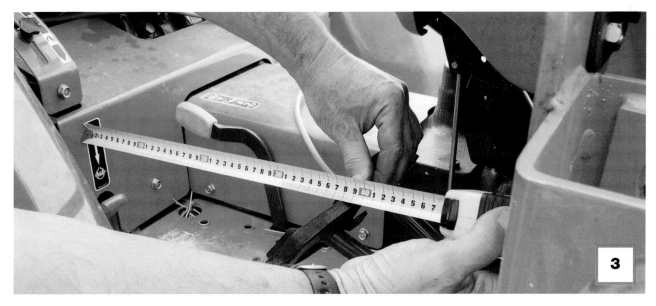

Press on the brake pedal with your hand until you feel resistance and measure the distance.

unlocked. Greasing the pivot shafts and working the brakes a number of times freed up the shaft and operation returned to normal.

On another tractor in this book, unlocking the brakes showed that one brake was not working at all. It turned out that part of the brake rods had broken near the brake itself, so that part had to be repaired.

4. If adjustments are needed, adjust the brake linkage on each side to get the free play within correct limits. For this tractor, the length of the rods are adjusted by loosening the lock nut, turning the rod to lengthen or shorten it, and retightening the lock nut.

5. On other tractors, free play is set with an external adjuster closest to the brake/rear end, and the rods on each side need to be set to the same length. Examine your tractor's brake linkage—if there appears to be a brake adjuster near the brake, use that to set the free play. If in doubt, consult the manual, the tractor dealer, or other owners for details on the procedure for your tractor.

The length of the rods on this tractor are adjusted by loosening the lock nut and turning the rod to lengthen or shorten it.

6. Once adjustment for each pedal is complete, lock the brakes together again. Drive the tractor and test brake operation together and individually.

A brake adjuster near the axle is used on this tractor to set the free play of the brakes.

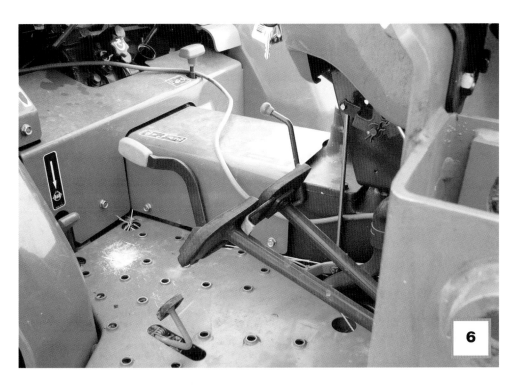

Lock the brakes together after the adjustments are complete.

For tractors with hydraulic activation, the place for making adjustments will look something like this. Have an assistant press the brakes while you observe what moves. The adjustment procedure is fairly similar to the project outlined below.

FUNCTIONALITY

115

PROJECT 24	Clutch Adjustment

Time: 1/2 hour or less

Frequency: Every 100 hours/yearly

Tractor specs needed: Clutch free play and where to measure it

Special parts: None

Special tools: None

Information needed: Clutch free play specification

Materials: None

Cost: None

Skill level: Moderately difficult

Tip: While adjusting the clutch underneath the tractor, lubricate the pedal pivot so that it operates freely.

Maintenance tip: Check clutch free play more frequently if the tractor is used for a lot of stop-start work or if heavy loads are frequently being hauled, both of which make the clutch lining wear faster.

Above and next page: *Some tractors are equipped with a spring-loaded catch to lock the clutch in a disengaged position. The reason for this catch is that when the tractor is left unused for long periods of time (e.g., in winter storage), clutch plates can rust together and become very difficult to disengage. Locking the clutch prevents it from sticking. Some owners of tractors without a catch simply use a long stick to hold the clutch open when the tractor is idle for months or years.*

Tractor clutch pedals need periodic inspection and adjustment of free play, which is the distance you can push the pedal with finger pressure before you feel strong resistance as the clutch disengages.

Too much free play means the clutch does not fully disengage, which creates harsh gear shifts and increased wear on the transmission. Too little free play means the clutch slips, preventing full power flow to the transmission and making the clutch wear out too quickly.

Tractor clutches are fairly easy to adjust because tractors of the era covered by this book usually use mechanical activation. If you've ever adjusted hand brakes on a bicycle, the process will be familiar—it's just on a much larger scale. On tractors, a rod from the clutch pedal pulls on the clutch disengaging mechanism. Adjusting the length of the rod adjusts free play.

TWO-STAGE CLUTCHES

Many tractors have a two-stage clutch, which means pushing the clutch about halfway down (first stage) interrupts power flow to the transmission, but still allows power to flow to the power take-off (PTO). Pressing the clutch pedal all the way down (second stage) stops power to the PTO. The reason for this system is that it allows the operator to stop forward travel while allowing a PTO-driven implement (e.g., a baler) to work through a tough spot.

You'll need to consult the manual for how to adjust the second stage. However, unless the clutch is badly out of adjustment (or a newly installed unit), adjusting the first stage free play as described below will probably be sufficient.

1. Park the tractor on level ground, remove the keys, and block the wheels so the tractor does not roll accidentally. Measure from some convenient fixed point to the face of the clutch pedal in its normal resting position and record the measurement.

2. Press on the clutch pedal by hand until you feel firm resistance as the clutch disengages. Measuring from the same point as in step 1, record the distance to the face of the pedal.

After the wheels are secured and stable, measure the clutch distance at resting position.

Press the clutch in by hand until you feel resistance and measure the distance.

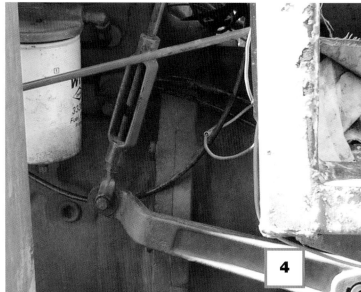

Turn the adjuster on this tractor to adjust the clutch.

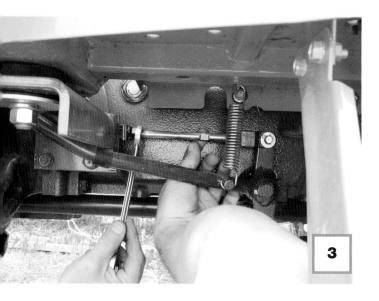

Free play is adjusted via the lock nut on this tractor.

Free play on this tractor is set by measuring the distance between the block and the clutch pedal stop.

3. On this tractor, free play is adjusted by loosening the lock nut, turning the rod to lengthen or shorten it, and retightening the lock nut.

4. A similar adjustment is made on this Case tractor by turning the adjuster.

5. On other tractors, free play may be set by measuring the distance between the block and the clutch pedal stop (shown where the screwdriver is inserted in the photo). The bolt that clamps the arm to the clutch shaft is loosened, the shaft is rotated to the disengagement point by pushing on a punch set in a bolt hole, and then the arm is retightened. Consult the manual or other owners for details on the correct procedure for your tractor. Once the adjustment is complete, drive the tractor and test the clutch operation, including second stage (if applicable).

PROJECT 25	Toe-in Adjustment

Time: 1/2 hour or less

Frequency: Every 100 hours/yearly

Tractor specs needed: Recommended toe-in

Special parts: None

Special tools: None

Materials: None

Cost: None

Skill level: Easy—the hardest part is taking the measurements

Tip: If one of the adjusting nuts seems particularly difficult to turn, don't turn it harder—you may be dealing with a left-hand thread, which turns the opposite direction. Spray on plenty of penetrating oil and give it a minute or two to work while you compare the threads to an ordinary right-hand thread bolt. Looked at from above, the threads on a left-hand threaded bolt slope down from left to right. A normal right-hand thread slopes up from left to right.

Maintenance tip: To maximize tire life, check toe-in when new front tires are fitted.

Maintaining the correct alignment of the front (steering) wheels of the tractor helps minimize tire wear. This is particularly important for front-wheel-assist tractors. A major tire manufacturer advises that the typical lug-bar R-1 tractor tire is especially sensitive to improper toe-in adjustment of the front end and wears more quickly if adjustment is off.

Toe-in means the distance between the centers of the tires is narrower at the front than at the rear. As the tractor drives forward, the front wheels bend back

After the tires are blocked and secured, measure the distance between the centers of the front tires, front and rear.

very slightly so a small "toe-in" at rest is used to ensure the tires run parallel in use. Wheel alignment on a tractor is much simpler than on a car or truck and can easily be done by the owner.

1. Park the tractor on a level surface with the steering wheel in a fairly straight-ahead position. If needed, drive forward a bit with hands off the wheel so the wheels return automatically to center. Remove the keys and block the rear wheels so the tractor does not roll accidentally.

Measure the distance between the centers of the front tires at the front and rear. To keep things consistent, measure the same height (e.g., hub height) front and rear.

A helper is handy for this, but if you have to do it alone and need a place to hook the tape, measuring from one side of a tire rib to the same side of the rib on the other tire is the same as measuring center to center.

2. If your sums indicate that the toe-in distance needs adjustment, locate the steering rod that has an adjuster. On this tractor, both lock nuts are loosened to allow the adjusting link to turn. The left side of the adjusting link side has a left-hand thread. Turn the link to get toe-in within specifications.

3. Another typical toe-in adjuster has a lock nut on one end and clamps on the other. The principle is the

This toe-in adjuster has a lock nut on one end and clamps on the other.

same—loosen both, rotate the link to adjust, and retighten.

4. Tighten the lock nuts and recheck the toe-in measurements to be sure it remains within specs—readjust if changed.

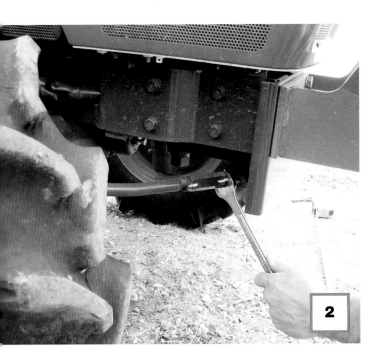

If the toe-in distance needs to be adjusted, find the steering rod that has an adjuster.

Tighten the nuts and measure the toe-in adjustment to see if it is correct.

<table>
<tr><td>

PROJECT 26

</td><td>

Install Block Heater

</td></tr>
</table>

Time: 1/2–1 hour

Frequency: One time

Tractor specs needed: None

Special parts: Block heater kit

Special tools: None

Materials: Pan, funnel, permanent-type (red) thread-locking compound

Cost: About $75

Skill level: Medium difficulty

Tip: If the tractor has coolant drain points only on the radiator, coolant may run out from the block when you remove the frost plug—have a pan ready to catch the runoff.

Maintenance tip: Avoid securing the block heater cord to any other electrical wiring or oil lines so that if the tractor is accidentally driven away with the block heater still plugged in, the line can rip free with minimal damage. Electric cords are easier to repair than ripped-out wiring or hydraulic hoses.

To maintain engine life and fuel efficiency, cold-starting (below freezing point) conditions need to be minimized. Most engine wear occurs in the first few minutes of starting a cold engine because cold oil thickens and resists flow to vital parts.

Cold conditions also put added stress on starting systems. A rule of thumb is that an engine is about five times harder to start at 0 degrees F than at 80 degrees F. Tractor batteries that have all of their power available at 80 degrees F will have only about 46 percent available power at 0 degrees F, so they are depleted faster, making the alternator work harder. The starter motor also has to work harder to overcome thickened engine oil.

An electric block heater raises the temperature of the engine coolant, which in turn warms the engine block and lubricants so the engine starts easier and reaches operating temperature faster. Block heaters are different than glow plugs, which only raise the temperature in the combustion chamber.

Using a block heater is a much more efficient and effective way to warm the engine than idling because idling contaminates engine oil more quickly. Oil contamination at idle is even more severe in diesel engines because the excess air in the combustion process cools the cylinder liners, resulting in incomplete combustion and condensation of unburned fuel on the cylinder walls. These deposits are eventually drawn into the engine sump where they contaminate the engine oil and reduce its ability to lubricate engine parts.

A block heater doesn't need to run up excessive electricity bills by being plugged in all night. Two to four hours (depending on engine size) is all that's needed to warm the engine sufficiently. An automatic timer can be used to switch on the block heater before you plan to start the tractor.

Locate a plug close the center of the block that has easy access.

121

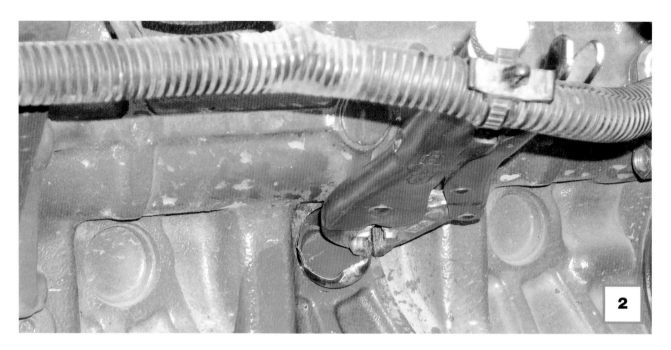

Grip the plug with locking pliers and pull to remove the plug.

1. The engine block will have a number of frost plugs (welch plugs), which are cup-shaped soft metal plugs held in the block by friction. If the coolant happens to freeze, the expanding ice can push the press-fit plugs out, preventing expensive damage to the engine block casting.

To install the block heater, one of these plugs (pointed out by the pencil) will be removed and the block heater will be installed in its place. Locate a plug on your engine close to the center of the block and that has easy access. For a more convenient way to install the block heater, the starter motor was removed on this tractor.

2. Using a punch and heavy hammer, tap on one edge of the plug to drive it toward the block. This will cause the opposite edge to rotate outward and allow you to grip it with locking pliers. Wiggle and pull until the plug comes out.

It is also possible to drill a hole in the plug and pry it out with a long punch, but this runs the risk of getting drill shavings in the coolant if you drill right through. To prevent contamination, drill until the bit is barely breaking through, then use a punch to enlarge the hole.

3. This block heater kit consists of three parts: the heating element, a steel sleeve to hold the element, and the electric cord. Before installing the block heater sleeve, permanent (red) thread-locking compound can be applied to ensure the seal.

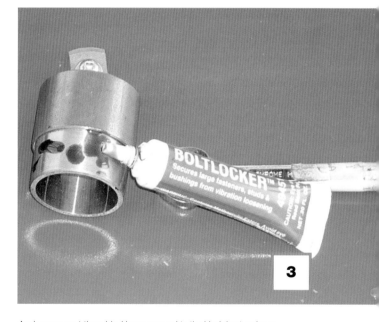

Apply permanent thread-locking compound to the block heater sleeve.

4. Set the sleeve squarely into the hole, and using a block of wood, tap it into position. Start slowly and check often to make sure it is staying square with the hole. Drive only as far as the instructions recommend, and in this case it is far enough to hold securely but not so far that it touches the cylinder walls. Feel inside to check that clearance is maintained.

Tap the sleeve squarely and securely in place.

5. Apply thread-sealing tape to the threads on the heating element and screw it securely into the sleeve.

6. Apply a dab of dielectric grease to the terminals and plug the cord into the heating element. Replace any engine components removed during installation, close the coolant drain points, and refill the radiator. Strain the coolant through a cloth or screen when refilling to prevent contamination.

Screw the heating element into the sleeve.

Dab dielectric grease onto the terminals and plug the cord into the heating element.

PROJECT 27	Add or Upgrade Headlights, Work Lights

Time: 1–2 hours

Frequency: As needed

Tractor specs needed: None

Special parts: Lights, switches if needed

Special tools: Wiring tools

Materials: Electrical tape, dielectric grease

Cost: About $20 per lamp added

Skill level: Medium difficulty

Tip: Work lights are available in either spot- or flood-beam patterns. Floodlights are useful for general work lighting, and spotlights are great for lighting particular parts of an implement you need to keep an eye on during work.

Maintenance tip: When replacing a halogen bulb, always handle the new bulb with clean gloves. A slight bit of grease on the new bulb's glass will cause premature failure.

Good headlights and rear- or side-facing work lights maintain a tractor's usefulness in a wider range of conditions. Along with brighter headlights in the existing holders, your tractor should be able to handle two or three additional work lights without straining the electrical system.

On dark winter evenings, you may have to rely on your tractor to push snow or pull vehicles out of the ditch. You may need to run an emergency electrical generator or the log splitter on a winter night. And sometimes it's just nice to be able use the tractor to pull a wagon for a winter night hayride.

Weather and breakdowns sometimes make field-work stretch into the night, and it is very stressful to keep the implement on track in dim light. Even if your tractor mainly works in daylight hours, there are other reasons to upgrade the lighting. Since the late 1990s, there have been huge advances in vehicle headlight technology, and those advances are a good upgrade for your tractor. Today's halogen bulb lighting makes the sealed-beam lights of the 1970s and 1980s look like jars full of fireflies by comparison.

1. To upgrade old round or square sealed beam headlights, remove the screws that retain the old headlight. Detach the electrical connector and take the sealed beam

with you to a tractor or auto supply store to find a brighter replacement.

2. For a new work light, choose a suitable position that won't interfere with safe operation. In this case, an existing hole in the fender was available. Scrape or use a

Codes in the headlight help determine a suitable replacement or upgrade.

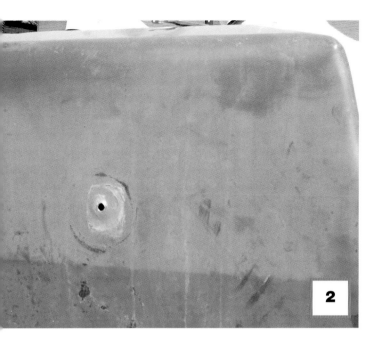

Clean the metal around the mounting hole.

Connect the lamp to the electrical harness.

wire brush to clean the metal around the mounting hole to enable a good connection to ground. Apply a thin layer of dielectric grease to prevent corrosion that could block the connection.

Caution: Do not drill mounting holes in the rollover protection structure (ROPS) because this may weaken the structure. Instead, use clamps to attach the light.

3. Figure out a place to connect the lamp to the electrical harness. Start by examining the tractor fusebox because it may already be prewired for work lights. If so, check the color of the wire going to that fuse location and see if the same color wire runs anywhere near your proposed work light position.

In some tractors, a work light circuit already exists, even though it was built with no work lights to keep the initial price lower. Check the fusebox for a colored wire that runs to a fuse position called "flood" or something similar and see if that same color wire runs near the proposed light location. You may find an lead ready for use, so pop in a fuse and test the circuit.

If there is no work light circuit, switch on the tractor headlights and use the test lamp to probe for which wires are "hot" when the headlights are on. You can use a scotch tap connection (see page 24) to take power from that wire.

After the wires are connected, test the light.

4. Using wire suitable for the load (see wire gauge chart on page 23), run wire to the proposed location. Use a little extra length so you have room for any final adjustments. Connect the wires and test the light. Secure all wire and connections so they are not dangling. Start and drive the tractor to make sure there is no interference with operation.

PROJECT 28 | Install Flashers for Road Travel

Time: 1 hour

Frequency: As needed

Tractor specs needed: None

Parts list: Flasher unit(s)

Special tools: Wiring tools

Materials: Electrical tape, dielectric grease

Cost: Varies with the type of flasher added

Skill level: Medium difficulty

Tip: The new range of LED flashers and bulbs are very bright and draw little current. However, their low power draw means your existing flasher located at the fusebox may not work properly, so you may need to replace it with one made to work with LED lighting.

Maintenance tip: Test operation every time you start the tractor so you can be sure they will work when needed on the road.

Today, one of the biggest hazards in farm operations involves moving tractors and implements along public roads. Like it or not, many car drivers do not pay sufficient attention to farm tractors (or much else). With the increase in high-speed vehicle traffic in country areas, there is an increased risk of collision with tractors. Whether or not the collision is your fault, it will certainly ruin your whole day and could involve you in an aggravating and expensive lawsuit. Flashers, reflectors, and slow-moving vehicle (SMV) signs help reduce the risk of collisions and country road rage and help show that you are safely operating your tractor.

The easiest solution for adding a flasher is to buy a Kojak light (above right), which costs about $35. The magnetic base sticks on a fender, and for power it plugs into a power point (see project 29 for installation instructions). The strobe beacon at left (about $50) has a powerful flash and can be hard-wired or fitted to a power point.

Good-quality, adhesive-backed reflective conspicuity tape is about $2 per foot and very bright when lit by headlights (as shown in the flash picture at right), and hard to miss in daylight as well. It's an easy way to increase outline visibility of implements and tractors.

A slow-moving-vehicle (SMV) sign, which costs about $10, is required at the rear on any slow-moving vehicle used on public roads.

1. Choose a flasher unit and plan out a suitable position for it. Note that this type of light does not flash automatically. Connected to a steady current, it will glow steadily.

Caution: Do not drill mounting holes in the rollover protection structure (ROPS) because this may weaken the structure. Instead, use clamps to attach the flasher.

2. Figure out a place to connect to the electrical harness. Since 1970, most tractors have been equipped with flashers, so you can connect to that wire or tap into the circuit with a scotch tap connector.

If no easy connection is apparent, connect a flasher unit (about $3) somewhere in the power supply ("hot") wire. A single flasher unit can run three to six lights—see package for specifications. In this case, one wire from the flasher is tapped into a headlight circuit wire, while the other goes to a switch controlling the flasher circuit.

If the ground connection for the light is being made through the tractor body or chassis, scrape or sand away sufficient paint for good ground connection. Smear a little dielectric grease on the exposed metal to prevent corrosion that could block the connection.

Connect the wires and test the flasher. Secure all wires and connections so they are not dangling. Start and drive the tractor to make sure there is no interference with operation.

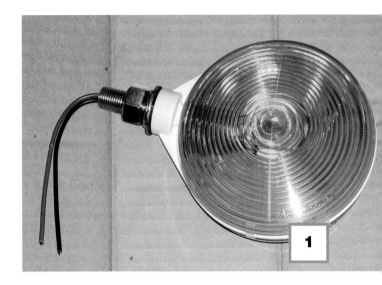

Choose the type of flasher unit you want on your tractor.

3a, b. If you are pulling wide, sight-blocking loads, such as a bale wagon, make sure drivers approaching from the rear can see the flashers. If necessary, mount the flashers on a long bar to extend visibility.

This tractor, for example, shows how a pivoting bar can be used to extend flashers with wide loads. A similar, though perhaps less elegant, pivoting bar could be made for older tractors.

Find a place to connect the existing flasher circuit, or purchase a flasher unit and use crimp-on connectors to wire it into the hot wire of the light circuit.

Make sure that your flashers are visible if you are pulling a wide and/or high load.

This tractor has a pivoting bar to extend its flashers.

| **PROJECT 29** | Install a 12-volt Power Point (Cigarette Lighter Receptacle) |

Time: 1/2–1 hour

Frequency: One time

Tractor specs needed: None

Special parts: Power point, inline fuse holder

Special tools: Drill bit big enough to make hole for the receptacle; wiring tools

Materials: Electrical tape

Cost: About $20

Skill level: Easy

Tip: Wire the receptacle directly to the battery terminals, so that it remains connected even when the key is turned to "off." This allows the connection of a battery trickle-charger through the power point.

Maintenance tip: Get a fuse holder that uses the same type of fuse as the others in the tractor (i.e., round glass tube or blade-type) so you don't have to carry two different kinds.

Although their use as cigarette lighters is going the way of the spittoon, the cigarette lighter receptacle, or power point as it's now called, remains a very useful maintenance upgrade. It provides convenient power for electrical accessories such as emergency flashers, cell phone chargers, GPS units, or a beverage warmer. In addition, it provides a quick attachment for a battery trickle-charger or electrical-system monitor.

1. Choose a convenient location for the plug. Check underneath or behind the proposed location to make sure you won't accidentally drill into something important. If flashers are being operated through this connection, it may be handy to mount the plug on the fender rather than the instrument panel. In this case, mounting it near the toolbox provides a secure place for a cell phone while it is charging.

2. On this tractor, an existing hole for the rear lights was exactly the right size (1-1/8-inch diameter) once the large grommet was pried out. The wires were long enough to be safely routed around the fender. If there isn't an existing hole, drill the hole with a suitable size bit or hole saw. If you don't have a big enough bit, you can trace the outline of the hole and cut it out with a small rotary grinder.

3. Remove the large retaining nut on the receptacle. Insert the receptacle into the hole and slide the nut over the wires and tighten the nut securely.

4. Route the wires to the battery location. Use grommets or wire sheathing wherever wires pass through sheet metal so that sharp edges do not rub through wire insulation and cause a short circuit.

5. To protect the receptacle circuit, use an inline fuse holder on the positive (red) wire. Using butt connectors, connect one end of the fuse holder to the positive wire

This receptacle with a spring-loaded weather cap is meant for mounting in a pickup bed or other location exposed to dust and moisture, which makes it a good choice for use on a tractor. Other types are available with rubber plugs.

FUNCTIONALITY

and the other end to a wire going to the positive terminal of the battery. Insert a fuse in the holder. A 5- or 10-amp fuse should be sufficient.

Crimp on ring terminals of appropriate size to wire ends and attach the ring terminals to the battery terminals. Use dielectric grease to prevent corrosion.

6. The receptacle is securely in place and hooked up.

7. Test that the receptacle can supply current. This inexpensive solid-state monitor confirms power, as well as gives an instant indication of battery and charging-system condition.

Insert the receptacle into the hole, slide the nut over the wires and tighten.

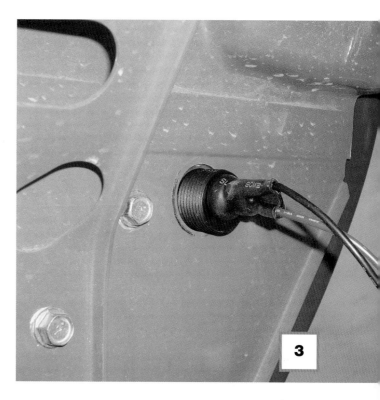

Select a location for the plug.

Route the wires to the battery.

If there isn't an existing hole, drill a hole, but make sure there is nothing behind where you plan to drill.

Use an inline fuse holder to protect the receptacle circuit.

5

Here is the receptacle in place and connected.

6

7

Test the receptacle to make sure it works.

132

PROJECT 30	Install Toolbox

Time: 1/2–1 hour

Frequency: One time

Tractor specs needed: None

Special parts: Suitable toolbox

Special tools: None

Materials: Metal, bolts

Cost: $5 and up, depending on toolbox

Skill level: Medium difficulty due to making brackets

Tip: Tape small or fragile items like fuses and cotter pins to the underside of the lid where they won't get covered up or broken.

Maintenance tip: Try to mount the box in a way that weight inside the box does not bend the sides. This will make it difficult to open and increase the risk of cracking. Mounting holes that are located in the bottom or near the ends reduce this problem.

To keep the initial price down, many tractors did not come with a toolbox. Adding one keeps often-needed items within reach and in a convenient location. It's also a benefit in terms of safety. The last thing you need when you have to suddenly operate a foot pedal or hand lever is to have a tool blocking the way!

With a well-maintained tractor, tools are more-often needed at the implement end of the tractor than near the engine. A toolbox at the rear also keeps implement hitch pins and three-point adjusting-link wrenches right where they are needed.

1. Choose a location for the toolbox, taking into consideration what's likely to be needed from it and that it can't interfere with access to other parts of the tractor. In this case, a spot just behind the seat looked promising.

Simple L-shaped mounting brackets can be bent in the shop, or as in this case, a shelf can be made.

Lock washers and thread-locking compound make sure the mount stays secure with the considerable vibration and jolting from the rough fields. A brace runs down diagonally to just above the red TDH-oil filler plug at the bottom for vibration control.

2. Check the fit. The mounting point needs to be far enough away from fenders, frame rails, etc., for the lid to open.

Choose a location for the toolbox.

3. The toolbox is securely mounted near the hitch end of the tractor. The SMV (slow moving vehicle) sign partially blocks access when reattached, but it's a good balance between that and placing the toolbox in an inconvenient place.

Make sure the toolbox fits and can open.

The toolbox is now fully attached.

Replacement hydraulic hoses with the correct fittings and length can be made on the spot at tractor shops and industrial supply stores. This crimping machine attaches fittings in seconds.

Dealers also offer toolbox kits. In this type, a special bracket is bolted to the frame.

The toolbox then simply clips onto the bracket and allows easy detachment for service tasks or to prevent theft.

CHAPTER 7
TROUBLESHOOTING

The following troubleshooting guide is limited to problems that the average maintenance person can remedy based on projects in this book. If none of these remedies solve the problem, you'll need to have a tractor repair shop look into some deeper problems. But being able to tell them what you've checked so far will save them valuable diagnostic time.

ENGINE

Will not crank.

1. Transmission or PTO safety interlock
    Shift transmission, speed range levers, and PTO to neutral.
2. Clutch safety interlock
    Press clutch pedal down.
3. Seat safety interlock
    Put full weight on seat.
4. Dead or weak battery
    Service the battery.
5. Wiring problems blocking current from battery
    Find and repair any loose connections, broken wires, or short circuits.
6. Faulty starter switch
    Try starting by connecting a remote starter switch. Use a multimeter to test resistance between switch terminals that go to the battery and to the starter. When the switch is turned to "start," the ohm reading should be near zero.
7. Faulty starter motor and/or solenoid (starter engagement switch atop starter)
    Remove solenoid and starter and have them tested at a repair facility.

Cranks, but will not start.

1. Fuel shutoff knob pulled out (diesel engine)
    Push knob to "run" position.
2. Choke not closed (gasoline engines)
    Move choke control to "start" position.
3. Battery too weak to crank engine fast enough
    Service and charge battery.
4. Fuel outlet tap turned off
    Open tap.

5. No fuel in tank
    Fill fuel tank.
6. Air in fuel lines (diesel engine)
    Bleed air from filters and injection lines.
7. No spark (gasoline engine)
    Service spark plugs and ignition points.
8. Air filter blocked
    Clean air filter.
9. Fuel filters blocked
    Change fuel filters.
10. Exhaust outlet blocked
    Clear blockage.

Starts, but runs roughly.

1. Wrong fuel in tank—diesel in gasoline or vice versa.
    Drain tank and fill with correct fuel.
2. Choke not open (gasoline engines)
    Move choke control to "run" position.
3. Not enough fuel in tank
    Fill fuel tank.
4. Water and/or sediment in tank
    Drain sediment bowl or trap.
5. Air in fuel lines (diesel engine)
    Bleed air from filters and injection lines.
6. Carburetor mounting bolts loose (gasoline engines)
    Tighten bolts.
7. Mixture screws improperly adjusted (gasoline engines)
    Adjust screws one at a time for smoother running.
8. Fuel filters clogged
    Change fuel filters.
9. Weak spark (gasoline engine)
    Service spark plugs and ignition points.
10. Exhaust outlet blocked
    Clear blockage.

Starts, but runs only for a short time.

1. Not enough fuel in tank
    Fill fuel tank.
2. Fuel flow blockage
    Change fuel filters.
    Clean out fuel supply line and tank.
3. Stuck float valve flooding carburetor (gasoline engines)

Rap carburetor with screwdriver handle to free valve.

Service carburetor.

4. Fuel tank air lock (gasoline engines)
Fuel cap vent clogged. Check if engine runs better with cap loose and if it does, replace cap.

5. Plugged air vent not allowing air into tank
Clean vent.

Starts, but will not develop full power.

1. Throttle control not opening fully
Adjust throttle-control linkage.

2. Clogged fuel filters
Change fuel filters.

3. Clogged air filter
Clean precleaner.
Clean air filter.
Tighten any loose connections on air filter intake pipe.

Overheating

1. Radiator dust screen clogged
Clean off screen to enable flow of air.

2. Coolant low
Check level.

3. Fan belt loose
Adjust belt tension.

4. Radiator cap not holding pressure
Replace radiator cap.

5. Thermostat stuck in closed position
Replace thermostat.

6. Radiator core is plugged
Examine core, flush, and refill coolant.

7. Engine overloaded, running at too low speed
Use a lower gear and higher engine revolutions.

Excessive fuel consumption

1. Clutch slippage
Adjust clutch free play.

2. Ballasting incorrect
Measure tire slippage and adjust ballast.

3. Fuel leakage
Repair hose and gasket leaks.

TRACTOR

Does not drive smoothly.

1. "Hops" under power
Check slippage and adjust ballast.
Implement load may be too heavy for tractor weight.

2. "Lopes" at road speed
Tire inflation incorrect—check and adjust.

3. Hard to steer
Grease steering linkage.
Make sure differential lock is disengaged.
Check and adjust front wheel toe-in.
Implement load may be too heavy for tractor.
Front wheels too light—adjust ballast.

4. Harsh ride
Check tire inflation.
Adjust seat.

5. Pulls to one side when braking
Adjust brakes.

Hydraulic operation slow

1. Hydraulic speed-control regulator setting
Adjust valve for desired speed of operation.

2. Hydraulic-oil level low
Check and fill to proper level.
Check and fill external hydraulic-fluid reservoir.

KEEPING IT TOGETHER

Bolts and screws coming loose on their own because vibration and heating—both of which your tractor have in ample supply—cause many operating troubles. Periodically going over the tractor and tightening the bolts and screws is good preventative maintenance. Along with preventing things from failing and/or falling off, it also prevents many annoying rattles and buzzes.

There are several ways you can keep pesky bolts, nuts, and screws tight without constant wrenching and prevent parts from continually loosening, causing annoying rattles, or falling off entirely.

• Use flanged bolts or nuts, which are now considered to be a top choice in the industry. The teeth on the flanges provide the locking ability.

• Use locking nuts, which have an insert to grip the bolt. Locking nuts should be used no more than three times before being replaced.

• Use lock washers, which are used underneath the bolt head or the nut. Spring-type lock washers were the traditional solution, but toothed washers are now considered a better choice.

• Make repairs with locking compounds, available in liquid, gel, or paste. Use blue (medium strength) compound for parts that need to be sometimes detached, and red (high strength) for parts, such as studs and bearings, that will rarely, if ever, be taken off again.

Top row, from left to right: KEPS nut with integral star washer; WhizLok flange nut with teeth on the flange to grip metal, which is excellent for sheet metal nut; with captive lockwasher. Bottom row, from left to right: external-tooth star washer, internal-tooth star washer, and old-tech spring lock washer.

Jam nuts are simply two regular nuts of the same size threaded onto a bolt or threaded shaft. The two nuts are turned together in opposite directions so that they jam together to prevent loosening. They work well.

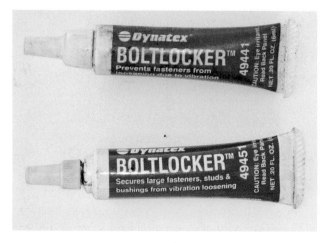

Thread-locking compounds are available in liquid (shown), gel, and stick. Blue compound is medium strength for fasteners that might have to be removed. High-strength red compound is for more permanent installations, such as studs and bearings.

APPENDICES

PART SOURCES BY ITEM
— Provided by Robert Pripps, compiled by Andrea Pripps

CARBURETORS

Burrey Carburetor Service
12426 Clayton Road
Monroeville, IN 46773
800/287-7390
info@burreycarb.com
www.burreycarb.com

Dengler Tractor Inc.
6687 Shurz Road
Middletown, OH 45042
513/423-4000
denglertractor@aol.com
www.denglertractor.com
Accepts Visa, MasterCard, Discover, American
    Express, FarmPlan

Dennis Carpenter
Ford Tractor Reproductions
4140 Concord Parkway South
Concord, NC 28027
704/786-8139
info@dennis-carpenter.com
www.dennis-carpenter.com

Denny's Carb Shop
Tractor Products
8620 N. Casstown-Fletcher Road
Fletcher, OH 45326-9786
937/368-2304
dennyscarbshop@ameritech.net
www.dennyscarbshop.com
Offers electronic ignition to replace points in most
    distributors for all makes of tractors for 6-volt
    positive, 12-volt positive, and 12-volt negative
    ground systems

Johnson Implement
6530 Maple Grove Rd.
Cloquet, MN 55720
218/729-7143
www.greenpart.com
Large inventory of new and old stock; two-cylinder
    John Deere tractor parts

J. P. Tractor Salvage
1347 Madison 426
Fredericktown, MO 63645
573/783-7055
parts@jptractorsalvage.com
www.jptractorsalvage.com
International/Farmall 1939 and up; host of the only
    Cub/Cub Cadet–only tractor show, "J.P.'s
    Midwest Cub-Arama," last weekend in September
    in Fredericktown, MO, held annually

Link's Carburetor Repair
P.O. Box 181
8708 Floyd Highway North
Copper Hill, VA 24079
540/929-4519 daytime
540/929-4709 after 7 p.m.
laurandy@swva.net
www.swva.net/linkscarb
Specialty: John Deere

Motec Engineering
7342 West State Road 28
Tipton, IN 46072
765/963-6628
motecengr@aol.com
Carburetors stock for all tractors; LP carburetors and
    regulators for all tractors; governors, wiring
    harnesses, and parts for MM only

Robert's Farm Equipment & Tractor Parts Inc.
11377 State Route 177 & 732
Camden, OH 45311
800/367-8751
Tparts2@cs.com
www.robertstractor.com
Over 4,500 tractors dismantled since 1939; used,
    rebuilt, and new replacement parts available;
    worldwide shipping

Taylor Equipment Company
3694 2 Mile Road
Sears, MI 49679
231/734-5213

Treadwell Carburetor Company
4870 County Highway 14
Treadwell, NY 13846
607/829-8321
Sells carburetor kits, repairs and rebuilds carburetors;
    carburetor modifications

Willard Equipment
2782 State Road 99 S.
Willard, OH 44890
419/933-6791
partsequip@yahoo.com
Sells industrial equipment

Woods Equipment Company
2606 S. Illinois Rt. 2
PO Box 1000
Oregon, IL 61061
800/732-2141
www.woodsequipment.com

DECALS
AC Tractor Salvage
Bill Deppe
8480 225th Avenue
Maquoketa, IA 52060
abcdeppe@cis.net

Dennis Carpenter
Ford Tractor Reproductions
4140 Concord Parkway South
Concord, NC 28027
704/786-8139
info@dennis-carpenter.com
www.dennis-carpenter.com

Jorde's Decals
935 Ninth Avenue Northeast
Rochester, MN 55906
507/228-5483
decals@jordedecals.com
www.jordedecals.com

J. P. Tractor Salvage
1347 Madison 426
Fredericktown, MO 63645
573/783-7055
parts@jptractorsalvage.com
www.jptractorsalvage.com
International/Farmall 1939 and up

Maple Hunter Decals
P.O. Box 805
Riley, IN 47871
812/894-9759
maplehunter@msn.com

Oliver Decals
Lyle W. Dumont
20545 255th Street
Sigourney, IA 52591
641/622-2592
oliver@lisco.com
www.oliverdecals.com
Decals, ornaments, and reproduction parts; tractor
    restoration service

R-M Distributors—MM Corresponder
Gaylen Mohr
3693 M Avenue
Vail, IN 51465
712/677-2433
Publishes quarterly magazine on
    Minneapolis-Moline; also has decals

Robert's Farm Equipment & Tractor Parts Inc.
11377 State Route 177 & 732
Camden, OH 45311
800/367-8751
Tparts2@cs.com
www.robertstractor.com

Steiner Tractor Parts Inc.
1660 South M-13
P.O. Box 449
Lennon, MI 48449
810/621-3000
sales@steinertractorparts.com
www.steinertractor.com

Taylor Equipment Company
3694 2 Mile Road
Sears, MI 49679
231/734-5213

Willard Equipment
2782 State Road 99 S.
Willard, OH 44890
partsequip@yahoo.com
In the tractor business since 1959; also sells
    industrial equipment

Woods Equipment Company
2606 S. Illinois Rt. 2
P.O. Box 1000
Oregon, IL 61061
800/732-2141
www.woodsequipment.com

EXHAUST SYSTEMS
Oren Schmidt
2059 V Avenue
RR1 Box 56
Homestead, IA 52236
319/622-4388
Makes stainless steel mufflers for all MM tractors

GASKETS
Jim Van De Wynckel
21527 Port Road
RR #4
Merlin, Ontario, Canada N0P 1W0
519/689-4028
wynckel@attcanada.net

Lubbock Gasket & Supply
402 19 Street
Box 2154
Lubbock, TX 79408
806/763-2801
joy@lubbockgasket.com
www.lubbockgasket.com

Olson's Gaskets Inc.
3059 Opdahl Road East
Port Orchard, WA 98366
360/871-1207
info@olsonsgaskets.com
www.olsonsgaskets.com
Supplies engine gaskets for the obsolete market; old
    cars, trucks, tractor, industrial, and one cylinder

Taylor Equipment Company
3694 2 Mile Road
Sears, MI 49679
231/734-5213

GOVERNORS
Fossum Fords
10201 East 100th Street
Northfield, MN 55057
507/645-8095

N-Complete LLC
10594 East 700 North
Wilkinson, IN 46186
765/785-2309
tom@n-complete.com
cindi@n-complete.com
parts@n-complete.com
www.n-complete.com
N-Series Ford 1939–1964; sells a complete line
    of Ford tractor parts and also remanufactured
    Ford tractors

MAGNETOS
MagElectro Service
300 FM 2013
Friona, TX 79035
806/295-3682; 806/265-5106; 806/295-3855
txfireman92@yahoo.com
Magneto and carburetor parts, sales, and service;
    new and used tractor parts

Magneeders
8215 County Road 118
Carthage, MO 64836
417/358-7863
jack@magneeders.com
www.magneeders.com

Mark's Magneto Service
395 South Burnham Highway
Lisbon, CT 06351
860/877-1094
www.deschene.com/marksmagneto/
Rebuilt magnetos and parts

Morgan McDonald Carb and Ignition
1001 Commerce Road
Jefferson, GA 30549
706/367-4179
mmcdonald_c_j@yahoo.com
www.mcdcarbign.bigstep.com

Taylor Equipment Company
3694 2 Mile Road
Sears, MI 49679
231/734-5213

PISTON RINGS
Paul Weavers Garage
680 Sylvan Way
Bremerton, WA 98310-2844
360/373-7870 phone and fax
For all engines to 1980

RADIATORS
Dengler Tractor Inc.
6687 Shurz Road
Middletown, OH 45042
513/423-4000
denglertractor@aol.com
www.denglertractor.com
Accepts Visa, MasterCard, Discover, American
    Express, FarmPlan

Dennis Carpenter
Ford Tractor Reproductions
4140 Concord Parkway South
Concord, NC 28027
704/786-8139
info@dennis-carpenter.com
www.dennis-carpenter.com

J. P. Tractor Salvage
1347 Madison 426
Fredericktown, MO 63645
573/783-7055
parts@jptractorsalvage.com
www.jptractorsalvage.com
International/Farmall 1939 and up

N-Complete LLC
10594 East 700 North
Wilkinson, IN 46186
765/785-2309
tom@n-complete.com
cindi@n-complete.com
parts@n-complete.com
www.n-complete.com
N-Series Ford 1939–1964; sells a complete line
    of Ford tractor parts and also remanufactured
    Ford tractors

Omaha Avenue Radiator Service
100 East Omaha Avenue
Norfolk, NE 68701
402/371-5953

Robert's Farm Equipment & Tractor Parts Inc.
11377 State Route 177 & 732
Camden, OH 45311
800/367-8751
Tparts2@cs.com
www.robertstractor.com

SEATS
Speer Cushion Company
431 South Interocean Avenue
Holyoke, CO 80734
800/525-8156
speercus@netscape.net
www.speercushion.com
Seat cushions; comprehensive listing for antique as
    well as newer equipment; recovers or
    manufactures seats to customer specifications

SPARK PLUGS
Donald McKinsey
P.O. Box 94
Wilkinson, IN 46186
765/785-6284
Specializing in obsolete spark plugs; complete price
    list on 70,000 spark plugs; also has 6-volt electric
    fuel pumps

STEERING WHEELS/REFINISHING
AC Tractor Salvage
Bill Deppe
8480 225th Avenue
Maquoketa, IA 52060
abcdeppe@cis.net

Dengler Tractor Inc.
6687 Shurz Road
Middletown, OH 45042
513/423-4000
denglertractor@aol.com
www.denglertractor.com

Dennis Carpenter
Ford Tractor Reproductions
4140 Concord Parkway South
Concord, NC 28027
704/786-8139
info@dennis-carpenter.com
www.dennis-carpenter.com

Minn-Kota Repair Inc.
38893 County Highway 12
Ortonville, MN 56278
320/839-3940
320/289-2473
mert@minnkotarepair.com
www.minnkotarepair.com
All parts are made in the United States

TIRES
Dengler Tractor Inc.
6687 Shurz Road
Middletown, OH 45042
513/423-4000
denglertractor@aol.com
www.denglertractor.com

Dennis Carpenter
Ford Tractor Reproductions
4140 Concord Parkway South
Concord, NC 28027
704/786-8139
info@dennis-carpenter.com
www.dennis-carpenter.com

J. P. Tractor Salvage
1347 Madison 426
Fredericktown, MO 63645
573/783-7055
parts@jptractorsalvage.com
www.jptractorsalvage.com

M. E. Miller Tire Company
17386 State Highway 2
Wauseon, OH 43567
419/335-7010
millertire@bright.net
www.millertire.com
Hard-to-find tires in original tread designs

Robert's Farm Equipment & Tractor Parts Inc.
11377 State Route 177 & 732
Camden, OH 45311
800/367-8751
Tparts2@cs.com
www.robertstractor.com

TOOLS
M. E. Miller Tire Company
17386 State Highway 2
Wauseon, OH 43567
419/335-7010
millertire@bright.net
www.millertire.com
Hard-to-find tires in original tread designs

TP Tools and Equipment
7075 State Route 446
P.O. Box 649
Canfield, OH 44406
330/533-3384; or 800/321-9260
www.tptools.com
Everything for your restoration

WHEELS
Dengler Tractor Inc.
6687 Shurz Road
Middletown, OH 45042
513/423-4000
denglertractor@aol.com
www.denglertractor.com

Dennis Carpenter
Ford Tractor Reproductions
4140 Concord Parkway South
Concord, NC 28027
704/786-8139
info@dennis-carpenter.com
www.dennis-carpenter.com

Detwiler Tractor Parts
S3266 State Highway 13
Spencer, WI 54479
715-659-4252
detwiler@tznet.com
www.detwilertractor.com
Recovers from and rear factory round and flat spoke
   wheels; rebuilds front steel wheels

J. P. Tractor Salvage
1347 Madison 426
Fredericktown, MO 63645
573/783-7055
parts@jptractorsalvage.com
www.jptractorsalvage.com

M. E. Miller Tire Company
17386 State Highway 2
Wauseon, OH 43567
419/335-7010
millertire@bright.net
www.millertire.com

Nielsen Spoke Wheel Repair
3921 230th Street
Estherville, IA 51334
712/867-4796
All makes with spoke wheels

Robert's Farm Equipment & Tractor Parts Inc.
11377 State Route 177 & 732
Camden, OH 45311
800/367-8751
Tparts2@cs.com
www.robertstractor.com

Taylor Equipment Company
3694 2 Mile Road
Sears, MI 49679
231/734-5213

Willard Equipment
2782 State Road 99 S.
Willard, OH 44890
partsequip@yahoo.com

Wilson Farms
20552 Old Mansfield Road
Fredericktown, OH 43019
740/694-5071

Woods Equipment Company
2606 S. Illinois Rt. 2
PO Box 1000
Oregon, IL 61061
800/732-2141
www.woodsequipment.com

WIRING HARNESS
Agri-Services
13899 North Road
Alden, NY 14004
716/937-6618
agrisev@rochester.rr.com
www.wiringharnesses.com
Also sells battery cables and switches; offers
discounts for FFA and school tractor projects

The Brillman Company
2328 Pepper Road
Mt. Jackson, VA 22842
888/BRILLMAN (888/274-5562)
john@brillman.com
www.brillman.com

Part Sources by Tractor Brand
ALLIS-CHALMERS
AC Tractor Salvage
Bill Deppe
8480 225th Avenue
Maquoketa, IA 52060
abcdeppe@cis.net

FARMALL (see International)

FORD
Dennis Carpenter
Ford Tractor Reproductions
4140 Concord Parkway South
Concord, NC 28027
704/786-8139
info@dennis-carpenter.com
www.dennis-carpenter.com

Fossum Fords
10201 East 100th Street
Northfield, MN 55057
507/645-8095

N-Complete LLC
10594 East 700 North
Wilkinson, IN 46186
765/785-2309
tom@n-complete.com
cindi@n-complete.com
parts@n-complete.com
www.n-complete.com
N-Series Ford 1939–1964; sells a complete line
of Ford tractor parts and also remanufactured
Ford tractors

O'Brien County Implement Inc.
Highway 18 East
Sheldon, IA 51201
712/324-4871; 800/320-6224
obci@nethtc.net
www.obci.net

The Tractor Barn
6154 West Highway 60
Brookline, MO 65714
417/881-3668; 800/383-3678
tractorparts@tractorbarn.net
www.tractorbarn.net
Specializes in older tractors; call for a free catalog

INTERNATIONAL, MCCORMICK-DEERING, FARMALL

Bates Corporation
12351 Elm Road
Bourbon, IN 46504
800/248-2955
batescorp@batescorp.com
www.batescorp.com
IH, Case IH, Farmall only; specializes in new, used, and rebuilt tractor parts for International Harvester, Farmall, and Case IH including crawler and construction models

Berkshire Implement Company Inc.
P.O. Box 237
U.S. Highway 35 N
Royal Center, IN, 46978
574/643-3115
Serving since 1952; home of the IH museum

Carter & Gruenewald
P.O. Box 40
4414 Highway 92
Brooklyn, WI 53521
608/455-2411
cngcoinc@mailbag.com
www.cngco.com
IH, Cub Cadet, and Woods Equipment parts

J. P. Tractor Salvage
1347 Madison 426
Fredericktown, MO 63645
573/783-7055
parts@jptractorsalvage.com
www.jptractorsalvage.com

Little Red Tractor Company
124 Marion Street
Howells, NE 68641
402/986-1352; or 888/802-5782
glen@littleredtractorco.com
www.littleredtractorco.com

Sieren Reproductions
1320 Highway 92
Keota, IA 52248
309/698-4042
tesieren@iowatelecom.net

JOHN DEERE

David Geyer Fabrication
1251 Rohret Road Southwest
Oxford, IA 52322
319/628-4257
Sells hoods for all unstyled John Deeres and John Deere 430s; also does custom sheet metal fabrication

Detwiler Tractor Parts
S3266 State Highway 13
Spencer, WI 54479
715/659-4252
detwiler@tznet.com
www.detwilertractor.com

The Farmacy
N1878 State Highway 13
Medford, WI 54451
715/678-2224; 715/678-2640 fax

H&J Machining
6757 Highway 200
P.O. Box 126
Carrington, ND 58421
701/652-3299
jsimons@daktel.com
Complete jobber machine shop; head, block, connecting rod work, sleeving, and crank grinding

John R. Lair
The Fender Vendor
413 L.Q.P. Avenue
Canby, MN 56220
507/223-5902
Near original fenders for all John Deere A, B, and G row-crop tractors

Johnson Implement
6530 Maple Grove Rd.
Cloquet, MN 55720
218/729-7143
www.greenpart.com
Large inventory of new and old stock; two-cylinder John Deere tractor parts

Morgan McDonald Carb and Ignition
1001 Commerce Road
Jefferson, GA 30549
706/367-4179
mmcdonald_c_j@yahoo.com
www.mcdcarbign.bigstep.com

Ritter Repair
15664 County Road 309
Savannah, MO 64485
816/662-4765
Two-cylinder John Deere tractor repairs; repairs and
calibrates test two-cylinder injection pumps and
injectors/John Deere two-cylinder diesel tractors

Robert's Farm Equipment & Tractor Parts Inc.
11377 State Route 177 & 732
Camden, OH 45311
800/367-8751
Tparts2@cs.com
www.robertstractor.com

Shepard's Two-Cylinder Parts
John Shepard
E633 1150th Avenue
Downing, WI 54734
715/265-4988; 715/265-7568 fax
js2cypts@baldwin-telecom.net
www.shepard2cypts.qpg.com
John Deere M-MT-40-420-435 tractor parts

Sieren Reproductions
1320 Highway 92
Keota, IA 52248
tesieren@iowatelecom.net

Taylor Equipment Company
3694 2 Mile Road
Sears, MI 49679
231/734-5213

2 Cylinder Diesel Shop
731 Farm Valley Road
Route 2 Box 241
Conway, MO 65632
417/589-3843; 417/468-7000
jd2cyldiesel@parts.net
Rebuilds and services all diesel two-cylinder fuel
pumps; also inline P-series pumps

Willson Farms
20552 Old Mansfield Road
Fredericktown, OH 43019
740/694-5071

Woods Equipment Company
2606 S. Illinois Rt. 2
PO Box 1000
Oregon, IL 61061
800/732-2141
www.woodsequipment.com

MINNEAPOLIS-MOLINE

Jim Van De Wynckel
21527 Port Road
RR #4
Merlin, Ontario, Canada NOP 1W0
519/689-4028
wynckel@attcanada.net

Motec Engineering
7342 West State Road 28
Tipton, IN 46072
765/963-6628
motecengr@aol.com
Carburetors stock for all tractors; LP carburetors and
regulators for all tractors; governors, wiring
harnesses, and parts for MM only

R-M Distributors—MM Corresponder
Gaylen Mohr
3693 M Avenue
Vail, IN 51465
712/677-2433
Publishes quarterly magazine on
Minneapolis-Moline

Welters Farm Supply
14307 Lawrence Farm Road 2190
Verona, MO 65769
417/498-6496

OLIVER

Lyle W. Dumont
Oliver Decals
20545 255th Street
Sigourney, IA 52591
641/622-2592
oliver@lisco.com
www.oliverdecals.com

Decals, ornaments, and reproduction parts; tractor restoration service

Lynch Farms Oliver Parts
1624 Alexander Road
Eaton, OH 45320
937/456-6686

O'Brien County Implement Inc.
Highway 18 East
Sheldon, IA 51201
712/324-4871; 800/320-6224
obci@nethtc.net
www.obci.net

Zimmerman Oliver-Cletrac
1450 Diamond Station Road
Ephrata, PA 17522-9564
717/738-2573
www.oliverceltrac.com
Oliver Cletrac crawler only

RUMELY
Taylor Equipment Company
3694 2 Mile Road
Sears, MI 49679
231/734-5213

Willard Equipment
2782 State Road 99 S.
Willard, OH 44890
partsequip@yahoo.com

Willson Farms
20552 Old Mansfield Road
Fredericktown, OH 43019
740/694-5071

Woods Equipment Company
2606 S. Illinois Rt. 2
P.O. Box 1000
Oregon, IL 61061
800/732-2141
www.woodsequipment.com

REPRODUCTION PARTS, ALL TRACTOR BRANDS
AC Tractor Salvage
Bill Deppe
8480 225th Avenue

Maquoketa, IA 52060
abcdeppe@cis.net

Antique Gauges Inc.
12287 Old Skipton Road
Cordova, MD 21625
410/822-4963 phone or fax
Mechanical oil, amp, and temp gauges

Charles Krekow
270 520th Street
Marcus, IA 51035
712/376-2663
Radiator guards for unstyled John Deere; canvas curtains, etc.; John Deere H curtains and toolboxes

David Geyer Fabrication
1251 Rohret Road Southwest
Oxford, IA 52322
319/628-4257
Hoods for all unstyled John Deeres; hoods for John Deere 430; also custom sheet metal fabrication

Dengler Tractor Inc.
6687 Shurz Road
Middletown, OH 45042
513/423-4000
denglertractor@aol.com
www.denglertractor.com

Dennis Carpenter
Ford Tractor Reproductions
4140 Concord Parkway South
Concord, NC 28027
704/786-8139
info@dennis-carpenter.com
www.dennis-carpenter.com

Detwiler Tractor Parts
S3266 State Highway 13
Spencer, WI 54479
715/659-4252
detwiler@tznet.com
www.detwilertractor.com

J. P. Tractor Salvage
1347 Madison 426
Fredericktown, MO 63645
573/783-7055
parts@jptractorsalvage.com
www.jptractorsalvage.com

Lyle W. Dumont
Oliver Decals
20545 255th Street
Sigourney, IA 52591
641/622-2592
oliver@lisco.com
www.oliverdecals.com
Decals, ornaments, and reproduction parts

Minn-Kota Repair Inc.
38893 County Highway 12
Ortonville, MN 56278
320/839-3940
320/289-2473
mert@minnkotarepair.com
www.minnkotarepair.com
All parts are made in the United States

Panning Bros. Tractor Parts
25060 651 Avenue
Gibbon, MN 55335
800/635-0993; 507/834-9713 fax
panningbros@yahoo.com
Free nationwide parts location

TRACTOR RESTORATION SERVICE

Dan's Tractor Service
Dan Langy
13340 West Green Bush Road
Lena, IL 61048
815/369-2684

Fossum Fords
10201 East 100th Street
Northfield, MN 55057
507/645-8095

N-Complete LLC
10594 East 700 North
Wilkinson, IN 46186
765/785-2309
tom@n-complete.com
cindi@n-complete.com
parts@n-complete.com
www.n-complete.com
N-Series Ford 1939–1964; sells a complete line
of Ford tractor parts and also remanufactured
Ford tractors

Robert's Farm Equipment & Tractor Parts Inc.
11377 State Route 177 & 732
Camden, OH 45311
800/367-8751
Tparts2@cs.com
www.robertstractor.com

Rosewood Machine & Tool Company
Duane L. Helman, President
P.O. Box 17
6423 Kiser Lake Road
Rosewood, OH 43070
937/362-3871; 937/362-3872 fax
Custom cast parts

Steiner Tractor Parts Inc.
1660 South M-13
P.O. Box 449
Lennon, MI 48449
810/621-3000
sales@steinertractors.com
www.steinertractor.com

Taylor Equipment Company
3694 2 Mile Road
Sears, MI 49679
231/734-5213

Tired Iron Farm
19467 County Road 8
Bristol, IN 46507
574/848-4628

Willson Farms
20552 Old Mansfield Road
Fredericktown, OH 43019
740/694-5071

RESTORATION EQUIPMENT

E&K Ag Products
HC 3 Box 905
Gainsville, MO 65655
417/679-3530
ekag@webound.com
Sleeve puller specialists

Restoration Supply
96 Mendon Street
Hopedale, MA 01747
508/634-6915; or 800/809-9156

resto@tractorpart.com
www.tractorpart.com
Does not carry used parts

TP Tools & Equipment
7075 State Road 446
P. O. Box 649
Canfield, OH 44406
330/533-3384; or 800/321-9260
www.tptools.com
Everything for your restoration

SHEET METAL
Charles Krekow
270 520th Street
Marcus, IA 51035
712/376-2663
Radiator guards for unstyled John Deere; canvas
    curtains, etc.; John Deere H curtains and toolboxes

Dengler Tractor Inc.
6687 Shurz Road
Middletown, OH 45042
513/423-4000
denglertractor@aol.com
www.denglertractor.com

Dennis Carpenter
Ford Tractor Reproductions
4140 Concord Parkway South
Concord, NC 28027
704/786-8139
info@dennis-carpenter.com
www.dennis-carpenter.com

Detwiler Tractor Parts
S3266 State Highway 13
Spencer, WI 54479
715-659-4252
detwiler@tznet.com
www.detwilertractor.com
Used, rebuilt, and new replacement parts available;
    worldwide shipping

Fossum Fords
10201 East 100th Street
Northfield, MN 55057
507/645-8095

J. P. Tractor Salvage
1347 Madison 426
Fredericktown, MO 63645
573/783-7055
parts@jptractorsalvage.com
www.jptractorsalvage.com
International/Farmall 1939 and up

Midwest Tractor Tim
56632 177th Lane
Good Thunder, MN 56037
507/278-4302
alillo@hickorytech.com
Specializes in louver punching, special fabrication,
    welding, and repair

N-Complete LLC
10594 East 700 North
Wilkinson, IN 46186
765/785-2309
tom@n-complete.com
cindi@n-complete.com
parts@n-complete.com
www.n-complete.com
N-Series Ford 1939–1964; sells a complete line
    of Ford tractor parts and also remanufactured
    Ford tractors

Robert's Farm Equipment & Tractor Parts Inc.
11377 State Route 177 & 732
Camden, OH 45311
800/367-8751
Tparts2@cs.com
www.robertstractor.com

Steiner Tractor Parts Inc.
1660 South M-13
P.O. Box 449
Lennon, MI 48449
810/621-3000
sales@steinertractors.com
www.steinertractor.com

Willson Farms
20552 Old Mansfield Road
Fredericktown, OH 43019
740/694-5071

NEW, USED, AND RECONSTRUCTED PARTS BY STATE

COLORADO

Speer Cushion Company
431 South Interocean Avenue
Holyoke, CO 80734
800/525-8156
speercus@netscape.net
www.speercushion.com
Seat cushions; comprehensive listing for antique as well as newer equipment; can recover or manufacture seats to customer specifications

INDIANA

Bates Corporation
12351 Elm Road
Bourbon, IN 46504
800/248-2955
batescorp@batescorp.com
www.batescorp.com
IH, Case IH, Farmall only; specializes in new, used, and rebuilt tractor parts for International Harvester, Farmall, and Case IH including crawler and construction models

K&K Antique Tractors
5995N-100W
Shelbyville, IN 46176
317/398-9883
info@kkantiquetractors.com
www.kkantiquetractors.com

Motec Engineering
7342 West State Road 28
Tipton, IN 46072
765/963-6628
motecengr@aol.com
Carburetors stock for all tractors; LP carburetors and regulators for all tractors; governors, wiring harnesses, and parts for MM only

N-Complete LLC
10594 East 700 North
Wilkinson, IN 46186
765/785-2309
tom@n-complete.com
cindi@n-complete.com
parts@n-complete.com
www.n-complete.com
N-Series Ford 1939–1964; sells a complete line of Ford tractor parts and also remanufactured Ford tractors

IOWA

AC Tractor Salvage
Bill Deppe
8480 225th Avenue
Maquoketa, IA 52060
abcdeppe@cis.net

Dan Shima
409 Sheridan Drive West
Eldridge, IA 52748
563/285-9407
Ornaments, new and used parts, repair manuals, and books

Jerry Everitt Used Tractors & Machines
15158 Canoe Road
Volga, IA 52077
563/767-2175
jeveritt_sons@iowatelecom.net

Lyle W. Dumont
20545 255th Street
Sigourney, IA 52591
641/622-2592
oliver@lisco.com
www.oliverdecals.com
Decals, ornaments, and reproduction parts; tractor restoration service

O'Brien County Implement Inc.
Highway 18 East
Sheldon, IA 51201
712/324-4871; 800/320-6224
obci@nethtc.net
www.obci.net

Rock Valley Tractor Parts Inc.
1004 10th Avenue
Rock Valley, IA 51247
800/831-8543
www.rvtractorparts.com
Carry all types of parts for all models of tractors

Valu-Bilt Tractor Part
1301 N 14th Street
Indianola, IN 50125
888/828-3276

www.valu-bilt.com
Formerly Central Tractor

KANSAS
James Gall
3027 Kestrel Road
Reserve, KS 66434
913/742-2657

LOUISIANA
Tom Klumpp Equipment & Salvage
2605 Alfa Romeo Road
Basile, LA 70515-3132
337/432-5804; or 877/430-4430
tkequip@centurytel.net
All parts for all makes of tractors

MASSACHUSETTS
Restoration Supply
96 Mendon Street
Hopedale, MA 01747
508/634-6915; or 800/809-9156
resto@tractorpart.com
www.tractorpart.com
Does not carry used parts

MICHIGAN
Taylor Equipment Company
3694 2 Mile Road
Sears, MI 49679
231/734-5213

MINNESOTA
Fossum Fords
10201 East 100th Street
Northfield, MN 55057
507/645-8095

John R. Lair
The Fender Vendor
413 L.Q.P. Avenue
Canby, MN 56220
507/223-5902
Near original fenders for all John Deere A, B, and G
row-crop tractors

Johnson Implement
6530 Maple Grove
Cloquet, MN 55720
218/729-7143

www.greenpart.com
Large inventory of new and old stock; two-cylinder
John Deere tractor parts

Minn-Kota Repair Inc.
38893 County Highway 12
Ortonville, MN 56278
320/839-3940
320/289-2473
mert@minnkotarepair.com
www.minnkotarepair.com
All parts are made in the United States

Panning Bros. Tractor Parts
25060 651 Avenue
Gibbon, MN 55335
800/635-0993; 507/834-9713 fax
panningbros@yahoo.com
Free nationwide parts location

Worthington Ag Parts
6901 East Fish Lake Road
Maple Grove, MN 55369
888/845-8456
www.worthingtonagparts.com

MISSOURI
J. P. Tractor Salvage
1347 Madison 426
Fredericktown, MO 63645
573/783-7055
parts@jptractorsalvage.com
www.jptractorsalvage.com
International/Farmall 1939 and up

The Tractor Barn
6154 West Highway 60
Brookline, MO 65714
417/881-3668; or 800/383-3678
tractorparts@tractorbarn.net
www.tractorbarn.net
Specializes in older tractors; call for a free catalog

Welters Farm Supply
14307 Lawrence Farm Road 2190
Verona, MO 65769
417/498-6496

NEBRASKA
Little Red Tractor Company
124 Marion Street
Howells, NE 68641
402/986-1352; or 888/802-5782
glen@littleredtractorco.com
www.littleredtractorco.com

Omaha Avenue Radiator Service
100 East Omaha Avenue
Norfolk, NE 68701
402/371-5953
New and reconditioned parts; no used parts

OHIO
Dengler Tractor Inc.
6687 Shurz Road
Middletown, OH 45042
513/423-4000
denglertractor@aol.com
www.denglertractor.com

Denny's Carb Shop
Tractor Products
8620 N. Casstown-Fletcher Road
Fletcher, OH 45326-9786
937/368-2304
dennyscarbshop@ameritech.net
www.dennyscarbshop.com

Robert's Farm Equipment & Tractor Parts Inc.
11377 State Route 177 & 732
Camden, OH 45311
800/367-8751
Tparts2@cs.com
www.robertstractor.com

Willard Equipment
2782 State Road 99 S.
Willard, OH 44890
partsequip@yahoo.com
Sells industrial equipment

PENNSYLVANIA
Wengers of Myerstown
814 South College Street
P.O. Box 409
Myerstown, PA 17067
800/451-5240
t.s@wengers.com

www.wengers.com
The largest computerized inventory of the East Coast

SOUTH DAKOTA
Central Plains Tractor Parts
712 North Main Avenue
Sioux Falls, SD 57104
605/334-0021

WASHINGTON
Yesterday's Tractors
P.O. Box 160
Chimacum, WA 98325
800/853-2651
info@yesterdaystractors.com
www.yesterdaystractors.com
Has a large number of discussion forums; more than
    10,000 photographs online and 1,000 new
    classified ads per week; hundreds of articles and
    always adding more

WISCONSIN
Carter & Gruenewald
P.O. Box 40
4414 Highway 92
Brooklyn, WI 53521
608/455-2411
cngcoinc@mailbag.com
www.cngco.com
IH, Cub Cadet, and Woods Equipment parts

Detwiler Tractor Parts
S3266 State Highway 13
Spencer, WI 54479
715/659-4252
detwiler@tznet.com
www.detwilertractor.com

The Farmacy
N1878 State Highway 13
Medford, WI 54451
715/678-2224; 715/678-2640 fax

Pate Tractor Equipment
1323 South Boulevard
Baraboo, WI 53913
608/356-8005
Specializes in Minneapolis-Moline

Shepard's Two-Cylinder Parts
John Shepard
E633 1150th Avenue
Downing, WI 54734
715/265-4988; 715/265-7568 fax
js2cypts@baldwin-telecom.net
www.shepard2cypts.qpg.com

Strojny Implement Company
1122 Highway 153
East Mosinee, WI 54455
715/693-4515
tractors@dwave.net
Specializes in old tractor parts

REPAIR MANUALS, LITERATURE, CATALOGS, AND BOOKS

Dan Shima
409 Sheridan Drive West
Eldridge, IA 52748
563/285-9407
Repair manuals and books

Jensales Inc.
Tractor Manuals and Toys
200 Main Street
Manchester, MN 56007-5000
800/443-0625
jensales@jensales.com
www.jensales.com
Carries service, operator, and parts manuals

Little Red Tractor Company
124 Marion Street
Howells, NE 68641
402/986-1352; or 888/802-5782
glen@littleredtractorco.com
www.littleredtractorco.com

Primedia Business (formerly Intertec Publishing)
9800 Metcalf Avenue
P.O. Box 1291
Overland Park, KS 66282-2901
800/262-1954
bookorders@primediabusiness.com
www.primediabooks.com

Taylor Equipment Company
3694 2 Mile Road
Sears, MI 49679
231/734-5213

Valu-Bilt Tractor Parts (Formerly Central Tractor)
1301 N 14th Street
Indianola, IN 50125
417/589-3843; 417/468-7000; 888/828-3276
jd2cyldiesel@pcis.net
www.valu-bilt.com

Welters Farm Supply
14307 Lawrence Farm Road 2190
Verona, MO 65769
417/498-6496

Worthington Ag Parts
6901 East Fish Lake Road
Maple Grove, MN 55369
888/845-8456
www.worthingtonagparts.com

Yesterday's Tractors
P.O. Box 160
Chimacum, WA 98325
800/853-2651
info@yesterdaystractors.com
www.yesterdaystractors.com

CATALOGS
Agri-Supply
General Farm Supplies
P.O. Box 239
Micro, NC 27555
800/345-0169
www.agri-supply.com

Dave Graham
Parts and Literature
415 South Santa Fe Street
Santa Ana, CA 92705-4139
714/667-5060
film@costaloffsetprep.com

Stemgas Publishing Company
P.O. Box 328
Lancaster, PA 17608
717/392-0733
Steam and gas-engine show directory

Tractor Supply Company (TSC)
200 Powell Place
Brentwood, TN 37027
615-366-4600
www.mytscstore.com

Valu-Bilt Tractor Parts (formerly CT Farm & Country/General Country)

P.O. Box 3330
Des Moines, IA 50316
888/828-3276
www.valu-bilt.com
New and used tractor parts and farm supplies

LITERATURE
Blane Bolte

8621 180th Street
Walcott, IA 52773
319/381-3693
Hart-Parr and Oliver literature and information

GENERAL INTEREST
Broken Kettle Books

710 East Madison
Fairfield, IA 52556
bkettle@kdsi.net
General stock of used books; large stock of farm machinery, construction literature, and collectible paper of many kinds

BOOKS, PUBLISHERS
Krause Publications

700 East State Street
Iola, WI 54990
715/445-2214
www.krause.com

MBI Publishing Company/Voyageur Press

Galtier Plaza, Suite 200
380 Jackson St.
St. Paul, MN 55101
800/826-6600
www.motorbooks.com

CLUBS, NEWSLETTERS, AND MAGAZINES
ALLIS-CHALMERS
Old Allis News

Pleasant Knoll Press
10925 Love Road
Bellevue, MI 49021
269/763-9770
allisnews@aol.com

AVERY
B. F. Avery Collectors & Associates

14651 South Edon Road

Camden, MI 49232
www.horizonview.net/~kault195
Including "Wards twin row," "The General," "B.F. Avery," M-M Avery Models V, BF, BG

CASE
International J. I. Case Heritage Foundation

P.O. Box 081156
Racine, WI 53408
www.caseheritage.com
Case tractors, steam engines, and machinery

CATERPILLAR
Antique Caterpillar Machinery Owner's Club

P.O. Box 2220
East Peoria, IL 61611
309/694-0664
cat@acmoc.org
www.acmoc.org

FERGUSON
The Ferguson Club

P.O. Box 20
Golspie, Sutherland
KW10 6TE
United Kingdom
Tel: 01408 633108
lawrence@jamieson.force9.co.uk
www.fergusonclub.com
United Kingdom-based club for those interested in the work and inventions of Harry Ferguson, especially the tractors and implements produced as the "Ferguson System" from 1926 to 1966; journal is produced three times a year; Ferguson Brown, Ford Ferguson, Ferguson TE 20-20/30 Ferguson 35, MF35-65 and MP100 series

FORD
Ford/Fordson Collectors Association Inc. (F/FCA Inc.)

Jim Ferguson, Secretary/Treasurer
645 Loveland-Miamiville Road
Loveland, OH 45140
www.ford-fordson.org

N-News LLC

Rob Rinaldi, Editor
P.O. Box 275
East Corinth, VT 05040
infon@n-news.com
www.n-news.com

The N-News magazine is the source for all vintage Ford Tractors; information, tech tips, color photos, history, lore, and more

FORDSON
Fordson Tractor Club
250 Robinson Road
Cave Junction, OR 97523
541/592-3203
Of interest to collectors and restorers of Fordsons and those who like to "show" Fordsons

HART-PARR, OLIVER
Hart-Parr Oliver Collectors Association
Membership, Bill Meeker
2962 50th Avenue
N. Henderson, IL 61466
309/464-5343
www.hartparroliver.org
Oliver, Hart-Parr, and Cletrac

INTERNATIONAL HARVESTER
International Harvester Collectors Club Worldwide
Publisher-Harvester Highlights Magazine
1857 West Outer Highway 61
Moscow Mills, MO 63362
636/356-4764
www.ihcollector.org

International J. I. Case Heritage Foundation
P.O. Box 081156
Racine, WI 53408
www.caseheritage.com
Case tractors, steam engines, and machinery

Red Power Magazine
Dennis and Sallie Meisner, editors
P.O. Box 245
Ida Grove, IA 51445
712/364-1231
www.redpowermagazine.com

JOHN DEERE
Two Cylinder
P.O. Box 430
Grundy Center, IA 50638
888/782-2582; or 319/345-6060
memberservices@two-cylinder.com
www.two-cylinder.com

Green Magazine
2652 Davey Road
Bee, NE 68314-9132
402/643-6269
www.GreenMagazine.com
Monthly magazine for John Deere enthusiasts

John Deere *Tradition* Magazine
Ogden Publications
1503 Southwest 42nd Street
Topeka, KS 66609
785/274-4300
Official magazine of the John Deere Collectors Center

MASSEY/MASSEY-FERGUSON
Massey Collector's News & Wild Harvest
P.O. Box 529
Denver, IA 50622
319/984-5292
Bimonthly newsletter for Wallis, Massey-Harris, and Massey-Ferguson enthusiasts

MINNEAPOLIS-MOLINE
Minneapolis-Moline Collectors
c/o Loren Book
18581 600th Avenue
Nevada, IA 50201
515/382-6470
lgbook@midiowa.net
www.minneapolismolinecollectors.org
Information referral to members with expertise; club gives a grant to worthy restoration projects; applications due June 1 of each year; apply on web site

MM Corresponder
3693 M Avenue
Vail, IA 51465
712/677-2491
www.minneaplismolinecollectors.org
Quarterly Minneapolis-Moline magazine

RUMELY
Rumely Registry
Ellis Wellman
13827 Mayfield Road
Chardon, OH 44024-7919
440/635-5651
Maintains a registry listing 2,000-plus Oil Pull tractors

GENERAL INTEREST

Antique Power Magazine (Missouri City, TX)
Box 838
Yellow Springs, OH 45387
937/767-1433
patrick@antiquepower.com
www.antiquepower.com
Covers all makes and models of tractors

Engineers & Engines Magazine
118 N. Raynor Avenue
Joliet, IL 60435
815/741-2240

Gas Engine Magazine
Ogden Publications
1503 Southwest 42nd Street
Topeka, KS 66601
784/274-4300
rbackus@ogdenpubs.com
www.gasenginemagazine.com

The Hook Magazine
Box 16
Marshfield, MO 65706
417/468-7000
editor@hookmagazine.com
www.hookmagazine.com
Specializing in antique and classic tractor pulling;
The Hook has event coverage nationwide,
technical articles, puller profiles, coming events,
and extensive classifieds

Steam Traction Magazine
(formerly Iron-Men Album)
Odgen Publication Inc.
1503 Southwest 42nd Street
Topeka, KS 66618-1265
800/678-4883
rbackus@ogdenpubs.com
www.steamtraction.com

Successful Farming Magazine
P.O. Box 4536
Des Moines, IA 50336
800/374-3276
www.agriculture.com

MAINTENANCE SAFETY TIPS

Among adults, bypass starting (operator standing on the ground during the start) is the leading cause of tractor runover accidents. Being run over by the tractor or attached equipment accounts for about 16 percent of all agricultural fatalities and 5 percent of hospitalizations. Runovers are second only to tractor rollovers as a cause of death on farms.

On tractors with bad wiring, broken starter switches, weak batteries or starters, and/or missing or bypassed safety interlocks, many operators are tempted to work around these difficulties by jump starting or short-circuiting part of the starter wiring. Starting the tractor in this way can result in the tractor starting while in gear and suddenly running over the operator or bystanders.

If the key is broken or the starter switch doesn't work anymore, replacement ignition/starter switches are inexpensive and widely available from tractor and auto supply stores. Your life is well worth the minimal time and effort needed to install it. Installation is simple and consists of attaching the wires to the back of the switch and then finding a suitable mounting hole, often the same hole as the original switch.

Tractors usually have various safety devices built into the starting system to prevent unsafe start-ups. The transmission and PTO may have to be in neutral or the clutch may have to be disengaged before the starter is energized. Many newer tractors also have a seat switch that only allows starting with the operator's weight on the seat.

A 60-year-old farmer was killed when he started his tractor while standing on the ground to the left of the tractor or while standing on the side step of the tractor. There were no witnesses to the event, but it appears that the farmer was standing on the ground, holding in the clutch with his left hand, starting the tractor with his other hand, then letting out the clutch assuming the transmission was in neutral. The tractor originally had a safety switch built in to the transmission, but it had been bypassed by the previous owner of the tractor. The farmer was found trapped partially under the left rear wheel of the tractor, dead at the scene.

A 51-year old farm worker died from injuries received when he was run over by the farm tractor he was operating. Because a key had previously been broken off in the ignition switch and the switch had not been repaired, to start the tractor the driver used a screwdriver to create an electrical short between the tractor's battery and starter, an operation that required the worker to position himself directly in front of the inner right front wheel while reaching into the engine compartment. The tractor lurched forward, running over the driver, knocked down a bystander and veered toward a roadway before being stopped by another person. The Medical Examiner listed the immediate cause of death as multiple head and trunk injuries.

SAFETY PRECAUTIONS WHEN STARTING OR BOOSTING THE TRACTOR:

- *Disengage the clutch (on manual gear shift tractors).*
- *Take the transmission out of gear or place the range lever in PARK.*
- *If booster cables are used, connect them to the dead battery, not directly to the starter.*
- *Start the engine from the operator's seat with the starter.*
- *If the starter circuit is broken or inoperable, diagnose the fault and repair it properly. Do not use short-circuit methods.*

TOOL AND PARTS CHECKLIST

1/2-inch-drive socket set with sockets
    from 1/2 to 1 1/2 inches
1/4-inch-drive socket set
Aerosol antiperspirant
Anticorrosion washers
Antigel additive
Anti-seize compound
Baking soda
Battery hydrometer
Brush for cleaning parts
Brush-on electrical tape
Buckets
Bullet-type connectors
Butt connectors
Carburetor cleaning spray
Chalk
Chisels
Cleaning solvent
Compressed air
Coolant
Coolant hydrometer
Coveralls
Crimping pliers
Dielectric grease
Digital multimeter
Distilled water
Drain pan
Dust mask
Electrical contact cleaner
Electrical tape
Electrical-system cleaner spray
Engine oil
Exhaust system cement
Exhaust weather cap
Extreme pressure (EP) grease
Eye protection
Feeler gauge tool
Files
Fire extinguisher
Fuel container
Fuel filters
Funnel (gauze filter preferred)
Gasket scraper
Gasket sealer
Gasoline engine stabilizer
Grease gun
Grommets
Hand-cleaning soap/oil

Heat-shrink tubing
Inline fuse holder
Insulated clips
Insulated wire
Jack
Jack stands
Jumper wires
Large ball-peen hammer
Magnetic screwdriver
Masking tape
Measuring tape
Mechanic's gloves
Needle-nose pliers
Oil filters
Penetrating oil
Permanent marker
Permanent thread-locking compound
Pipe thread sealing tape
Pliers
Punches
Rags/towels
Reflective tape
Ring connectors
Rubber disposable gloves
Sawdust or cat litter for spills
Scotch-tap connectors
Screwdrivers
Set of combination (open-end and box-end) wrenches
    from 3/8 to 1 1/2 inches
Set of double ended wrenches
Silicone oven mitts
Soft mallet
Spade-type connectors
Spark plug gapping tool
Spark plug socket
Spark plug tester
Terminal puller
Test lamp
Thread locking compound
Torque wrench
Transmission-differential-hydraulic (TDH) oil
Wheel-bearing greaser
Wheel hub dust-cap removal tool
Wire brush
Wiring diagram
Wooden blocks (large, to block wheels)
Wooden blocks (small, use to protect parts while
    hammering)

INDEX

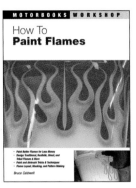

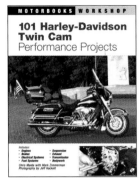
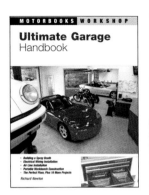